NIPPON SHINDO RON

OR THE NATIONAL IDEALS
OF THE JAPANESE PEOPLE

T0381652

YUTAKA HIBINO

NIPPON SHINDO RON
OR THE NATIONAL IDEALS
OF THE JAPANESE PEOPLE

by

YUTAKA HIBINO, LL.B.

(IMP. UNIV. TOKYO)

Founder of Ikuye Commercial College, Nagoya,
formerly Principal of First Government Middle
School, Aichi Prefecture, and Member of Parlia-
ment, Aichi Prefecture

Translated
with an Introduction
by

A. P. McKENZIE, M.C., M.A.

CAMBRIDGE
AT THE UNIVERSITY PRESS
1928

CAMBRIDGE UNIVERSITY PRESS
Cambridge, New York, Melbourne, Madrid, Cape Town,
Singapore, São Paulo, Delhi, Mexico City

Cambridge University Press
The Edinburgh Building, Cambridge CB2 8RU, UK

Published in the United States of America by Cambridge University Press, New York

www.cambridge.org
Information on this title: www.cambridge.org/9781107623217

First published 1928
First paperback edition 2013

A catalogue record for this publication is available from the British Library

ISBN 978-1-107-62321-7 Paperback

CONTENTS

INTRODUCTION

THIS Introduction is addressed primarily to foreign readers and more especially to those who have acquired as yet no great familiarity with the intimate aspects of Japanese life. The footnotes and the Appendix have been prepared with the same object. The Japanese reader will find little that is new or of interest unless he should happen to be a student of the more recent developments in the field of social psychology.

With the translation of the "Nippon Shindo Ron" a contribution has been made to the short list of original sources available in English to students of the social and political life of modern Japan. The importance of the book is due to the fact that it deals exclusively with conceptions with which every Japanese is familiar. The ideas set forth here form the groundwork and skeleton of the common intellectual life of the people. It is true that Mr Hibino has systematised these ideas and arranged them relative to the central conception of loyalty, but the ideas themselves are the common symbols about which are grouped the characteristic reactions of Japanese social behaviour.[1]

This point cannot be too strongly urged. The amazing phenomenon of Meiji Japan, a phenomenon which recent events have served to bring into still greater prominence, is not to be explained without an adequate knowledge of the ideals of the people as set forth in this book and other works of a similar nature. To the occidental reader many of these ideas may seem at first sight somewhat abstract or perhaps merely platitudinous. He should remember, however, that in politico-ethical writings of this kind the Japanese seem to prefer the abstract to the concrete. Sonorous repetition also appears to be more acceptable than concise argument. To the oriental conviction is the result of intuition and he is always inclined to rate the more subtle and immediate action of the mind higher than the laborious and

---

[1] The term "behaviour" is used throughout this Introduction in the technical sense.

obvious conclusions arrived at by those processes of logical argument so dear to the occidental. No considerable progress in the study of Japanese sources can be hoped for unless these points are kept continually in mind. It should not be forgotten that the characteristic behaviour of the greatest, the most progressive, the most virile, the most flexible and adaptable, and the most intelligent of Asiatic peoples is implicit in these apparently abstract symbolic conceptions. Upon this basis has been reared the fabric of a successful national assimilation of European and North American industrial devices and mechanical inventions, commercial enterprises with their necessary material adjuncts, the political and legal machinery of foreign countries, western educational methods, scientific achievements, and certain aspects of the more prominent religious and social theories of occidental civilisation. That mutual modifications in culture and in the basic group symbolisms are bound to occur, especially in the world of the Pacific, must be obvious to every thoughtful student, but it is not the province of this Introduction or of this book to deal with such speculations, attractive though they may be, except in so far as the text reveals the modifications which Japanese leaders themselves conceived as desirable in the course of the great Meiji period (1868–1912). To them it appeared necessary to make numerous secondary adjustments in the socio-political faith of the people. They saw clearly enough that the old class distinctions would have to be abolished. They realised also that the narrow nationalism of the Shinto revival of the eighteenth century would have to be revised before Japan could take her place in the comity of nations. These were insistent and difficult problems. A careful examination of the passages bearing upon them in this volume will enable the reader to understand the characteristic Japanese attitude towards many of these questions to-day. Sweeping and revolutionary though the outward changes may have appeared to the foreign observer a very little study will serve to show that the statesmen and educators of the period regarded them as important but secondary adjustments and alterations in the life of the people and as quite distinct from the primary and fundamental national ideals and institutions bequeathed to them by their ancestors.

With the abolition of class barriers it became necessary to enforce the obligations of the national ideals in a uniform manner upon all the orders. At the same time it was clearly seen that the new citizenry needed instruction in the nature and purpose of the adjustments and alterations already referred to. This was conceived to be one of the prime tasks of national education. The present volume was designed to serve this purpose for youths between the ages of twelve and eighteen. During the sixteen years that have elapsed since the close of the Meiji period there has been a tendency in official educational circles towards a still greater emphasis upon the characteristic national ideals. The present volume may be regarded, therefore, as a source-book for the great Meiji transitional period as well as an introduction to the study of Japanese behaviour at the present time.

The "Nippon Shindo Ron" is in no sense an abstruse volume addressed to the scholarly few. It is concerned throughout solely with those conceptions and ideals whose clear comprehension and practice by all members of the community is conceived to be essential for the healthy development of the national life. Such a book should be of peculiar interest to the student of political and social history, for no other nation has passed successfully through so many or such radical changes and in so short a space of time. It should be of use to the student of Pacific problems, for clear mutual understanding is of the essence of true progress towards the solution of many vexed questions. Thoughtful students in other Asiatic lands who may be desirous of discovering the basis of Japan's phenomenal success may find food for thought in its pages. A study of its teachings should be of interest also to the diplomatist, the journalist, the business man, the traveller, and to other students who have little time to pursue the more advanced studies which are now happily available in some profusion from the pens of eminent Japanese and foreign scholars and in the published researches of learned societies. To all such a knowledge of the factors which govern the common behaviour of the Japanese people is of considerable interest. There are two other classes of foreign residents in Japan for whom a careful study of original sources would seem to be of the highest importance. These are, respectively, the foreign teacher, employed in government or private schools, and the missionary, whether engaged in evangelistic, social, or academic work. The foreign teacher resident in Japan is sometimes in danger of overlooking the fact that he is in contact with the youth of the nation at the period of greatest familiarity with occidental ideals and theories and of the least concern with practical affairs. He is, therefore, apt to discount the power of the old symbolic group ideals set forth in this volume. That the missionary, the active propagandist of a new religious system, should devote the most painstaking care to the study of all the determinants of behaviour may seem obvious enough. It is as superficial as it is easy to claim that political behaviour and ethical behaviour are separable and that the Meiji government officially and formally recognised this distinction in setting aside the barriers hitherto maintained against foreign religious teachings. Two problems which still remain may be mentioned in passing. It is a question how far the general good of mankind may be advanced by an unimaginative effort to duplicate in the east determinants of behaviour which have evolved in a totally different setting, especially perhaps in view of the fact that the behaviour referred to seems to be undergoing radical modification in the countries of its origin. In the second place every serious and intelligent champion of a new creed must readily appreciate the fact that behaviour in all communities is closely dependent upon symbolism. It is undoubtedly true that the symbolic determinants of behaviour are of many kinds and that symbols may undergo mutual assimilation with advantage to both cultures. It is perhaps hardly necessary to add that this is the true goal of the practical humanitarian. Nevertheless, it should be borne in mind that the greatest tragedies arising out of cultural contacts have often had their origin in the unintelligent exchange of the symbolic determinants of behaviour. In authorising the present translation of his work Mr Hibino has expressed the hope that occidental peoples may thereby be made acquainted with those ideals which are primary and fundamental in the individual and national life of the Japanese people and upon which their characteristic behaviour is based.

In the course of the search for a concise statement of the revised politico-ethical faith of the people there was produced in 1890 one of the most noteworthy documents that have ever graced the pages of history. In some respects it is comparable with those remarkable ebullitions of the English-speaking peoples, the Magna Carta and the Declaration of Independence. In its intimate concern with individual and group behaviour, however, it surpasses both. This document is the Imperial Rescript on Education, known in Japan as the "Chokugo". Its noble and beautiful periods are familiar to every schoolboy for it is intoned with marks of respect and veneration at all important anniversaries and functions and in every grade and type of educational institution. It is a striking epitome of the political and social obligations of the Japanese subject. With its attendant symbolism it is probably the most important determinant of behaviour evolved in the Meiji period. In this brief formula the effort is made to link the new Japan with the old. It is also a remarkable and interesting attempt to make the symbolic ideas of a peculiar group common to all the orders of the new society. Although its very brevity is a serious barrier to the foreign student it deserves far more attention than has hitherto been devoted to it. The thirty chapters of Mr Hibino's "Nippon Shindo Ron" constitute an admirable commentary and exposition of the symbolic formulas contained in this Rescript. The titles of the several chapters are taken from it. In the present edition the translator has slightly altered the accepted English version with a view to bringing the titles into closer accord with the actual contents of the chapters. In his exposition Mr Hibino has summarised the whole socio-political faith of the Japanese people in so far as it is held by all. Those who desire to understand the determinants of behaviour provided by the makers of modern Japan for dissemination through the agency of the national schools would be well advised to study this volume. At the same time this "Way of the Subject"[1] provides the occidental reader with a comprehensive introduction to the inner meaning of the Rescript. Mr Hibino offers here a consistent and systematised exposition of the Rescript in so far as he has grouped the whole socio-political system about the symbolic idea of loyalty, thus disposing of the old controversy between filial piety and loyalty, a relic of the days when the letter of the Chinese classic was considered to be of paramount importance.

To the casual reader the inclusion of the article on the devotional self-destruction of General Nogi, the facsimiles of the correspondence regarding the printing of the marginal comments, and the comments themselves, which are in this edition placed in a special Appendix, may seem somewhat irrelevant. This apparent incongruity must disappear, however, as soon as the intimate relation between the General's symbolic act and the effective enforcement of the national ideals in the new society is realised. As the book indicates this was not always a simple task. The volume of foreign culture which poured into the country throughout the Meiji period produced naturally and inevitably crests of enthusiasm and revulsion. In the turmoil of wholesale social readjustment it was by no means easy to centre the attention of the new citizenry upon the old sanctions. True, these sanctions and symbolic formulas were already sufficiently familiar to the lower orders, but they were now challenged for the first time to regard them and to react to them in a manner which had hitherto been looked upon as the prerogative of an exclusive and dominant group. All the machinery of public education was not always sufficient to achieve these ends. In attempting to make general what had formerly been distinctive group difference tendencies the leaders of the Meiji period ignored or were forced by circumstances to neglect one very important consideration. It was impossible to conserve much

[1] The term "Shindo" means literally "Way of the Subject."

of the symbolism by which the dominant group had maintained its separate existence. The Meiji experiment was, therefore, in a sense an attempt to reproduce a special type of behaviour in the absence of a considerable portion of the symbolic background to which it had become attached. General Nogi's military exploits in the Russo-Japanese War placed him high in the public esteem. What is perhaps of more importance to the thesis of this book, he displayed both in private and public life the symbolic behaviour of the order to which he belonged in so far as it was consistent with the revised teachings of the national ideals. The circumstances attending the loss of his two sons and more especially the act of self-immolation in which he was joined by the Countess produced a profound impression upon the Japanese people and undoubtedly contributed to the crystallisation of popular sentiment in respect to the national ideals. With these considerations in mind it is not difficult to understand why Mr Hibino should have been at some pains to include in the later editions of his work an account of the highly symbolic act which crowned the General's career. That act emphasised in a dramatic manner the persistence of special group difference tendencies in the new social order. Nor is it surprising that the author has sought to record in the facsimiles of the General's letters and the spontaneous marginal jottings the warm approval with which he welcomed the main thesis of this book. Neither the letters nor the marginal comments which General Nogi inscribed with his brush while taking the cure at Shuzenji were intended for publication or for the eye of the author. Mr Hibino rightly feels that the circumstances under which these expressions of opinion were written add to their value. Although the marginal comments are frequently critical a glance will serve to show that the criticism is levelled at more or less trifling matters of detail such as figures of speech, illustrations, or rhetorical constructions which did not meet with the General's approval. His hearty acceptance of the main propositions is clear enough. Coming from the brush of the foremost exponent of the old group difference tendencies in the new social order

the inclusion of the material that has reference to General Nogi
will need no justification where the Japanese reader is concerned.
For the foreign student these three additions to the original
text are of considerable interest as they serve to indicate the
gradual crystallisation of public sentiment about the revised
national ideals so clearly in evidence since the later years of the
Meiji period. Whether it is possible to transfer the special
behaviour of a group to a much larger group without maintaining the original symbolism intact is a problem for the student
of social psychology. No other existing society can provide a
basis for such study comparable in interest and importance with
the material available in the social and political life of the modern
Japanese Empire. The present volume offers many indications
of the means by which the Meiji leaders sought to frame an
adequate solution for this difficult problem.

The author of this book, Mr Yutaka Hibino, retired from
active public life some years ago. He now spends much of his
time at the beautiful family seat which overlooks the teeming
thoroughfares and smoking chimneys of Greater Nagoya, the
industrial and commercial metropolis of "Central" Japan. The
spacious residence with its gracious old-world contours stands
in a park which crowns the first of the low hills which form the
eastern suburbs of the city. It has often been the privilege of
the writer to spend an evening with the author on the lofty
balcony of the audience chamber looking out over a garden
reminiscent of the days when men had leisure to devote to the
cult of natural beauty. In that garden are fine tennis courts, the
last word in modern construction and appointment, for Mr
Hibino, though over sixty years of age, is an ardent devotee of
sport. As the sun sinks behind the hills of old Yamato, cradle
of the Japanese nation, its last beams strike across the fertile
coastal plain whose rich and unfailing produce contributed in no
small measure to the greatness of the author's famous ancestor.
For a moment the light flashes from the golden dolphins which
crown the lofty tower of the noblest remaining relic of Japanese
feudal architecture. Farther to the south and almost in the exact

centre of the new city looms the exotic silhouette of the great
Hongwanji temple partly obscured by the factory smoke drifting
up from the bayside with the last breath of the day breeze
attracted by the latent heat of countless tile roofs and dusty
streets. Scattered in between are visible the uncompromising
outlines of chimneys and factories interspersed at intervals by
the tall bulk of a modern department store or office building. In
the gathering obscurity of the evening and almost in line with
the great castle which still guards the northern approaches to the
city stands the foremost Provincial Middle School of which the
author was for some years the distinguished principal. It was
during his tenure of office in this institution that the text of the
"Nippon Shindo Ron" was prepared. Somewhat nearer but
in the same general direction may be observed the new buildings
of the Ikuye Commercial Academy of which he is the founder.
Farther afield lies the important constituency which he repre-
sented for some years at the capital in a public capacity. Such
in brief is the scene of the author's active life. Here for many
years as educator and public man he has sought to enforce and
perpetuate the national ideals of a by-gone age. Here he has
sought to champion the best traditions of sport and athletics.
In early life he was of a weakly constitution. On the advice of
his physician he developed an interest in athletics, choosing
running as his particular hobby. He early made the classic
Marathon an object of special study and may fairly be said to
have introduced this race into Japan. Since his retirement from
active public life he has devoted a great deal of time and energy
to the encouragement of athletics and has written a popular book
entitled "Athletics from Practical Experience." The Marathon,
however, is still his chief delight. In conjunction with the recent
Olympic Games held at Paris he gave demonstrations in different
parts of Europe of the special "form" which he has developed.
At the moment of writing he is on his way from Japan to attend
the Olympic Games in Holland. He attributes his remarkable
vigour to constant practice in running and although well-
advanced in years he may still often be seen, equally indifferent

to summer heat and winter snows, leading a group of schoolboys or selected athletes in a long cross-country run over the plains of his native Aichi.

A word may be said regarding the translation. The original is written in the impressive, highly ornate, sonorous, and neatly balanced classical style so familiar to students of the older Japanese politico-ethical writings. In the opinion of competent Japanese critics it is a fine example of the style in question but its very merits make it the despair of the translator. Balanced repetition, the constant use of superlatives, and the splitting of compounds for the sake of rhythm and music render a close translation exceedingly difficult. To add to the trials of the translator there are, on the average, three to four difficult and important terms for each page of the original text which are not found in any Japanese-English dictionary. Recourse to a laborious analysis of the separate characters and comparison with other passages is then the only alternative. A constant rhetorical device is the splitting of compounds composed of characters of approximately the same meaning. Delicate nuances of meaning and emphasis are thus introduced into the original which cannot be reproduced adequately in translation. The only resort of the translator is to employ two different English words. As he cannot enrich his vocabulary at will by a convenient disintegration of the English compound the result is often a somewhat tedious repetition, while the verb, according to the canons of English composition, must be rendered in the plural. Of deficiencies arising from these sources the translator is only too conscious. Nevertheless, the attempt has been made to approximate as closely as possible to the balanced rhythm of the Japanese text. Wherever possible the flavour of the original has been preserved even at the cost of phrasing which may appear at times somewhat cumbersome and unusual. An attempt has also been made to reproduce the specific idiom wherever that can be rendered into intelligible English. Some alterations in tenses and sentence divisions have seemed imperative in the interests of clarity and the Japanese reader who may compare this translation with the original is asked to bear this in mind. With the full consent of the author the translator has freely elevated most of the important subordinate clauses of the involved classical construction to the dignity of separate sentences. In passing, a word may be said with regard to the familiar rhetorical device of superlative statement. The reader who has little acquaintance with Japanese or Chinese classical texts is liable to be misled by the apparently extravagant phraseology. There is a tendency in all such writings to state the ideal as though it were the actual. This is often nothing more than a rhetorical device employed for the sake of emphasis or inspiration, sometimes merely to give an appropriate ending to a long and intricate sentence or paragraph. In translation such clauses gain an undue prominence when set off in separate sentences. Students of the writings of the Shinto or nationalist revival of the eighteenth century to which the style of the present volume bears some resemblance will at once recognise the difficulty alluded to. This is not to deny, however, that the fervid patriotism of the later Meiji period, an epoch in which the nation was engaged in a life-and-death struggle with the resources of the Russian Empire, has led to superlative statements which an occidental with a different literary tradition might regard as extravagant. In any case the actual national achievements of the Meiji period were so amazing that some extravagance in statement would seem to be justifiable. After all has been said, however, it must be admitted that the sense of individual and group difference tendencies is exceedingly strong among the Japanese. It is natural that they should emphasise these differences and that they should attribute their substantial and noteworthy achievements to them. The thoughtful student will not be repelled by differences of literary standard in his study of the factors which have established the pre-eminence of Japan among the other Asiatic peoples.

The "Nippon Shindo Ron" was written by a Japanese for the stimulation and inspiration of Japanese youth and minute historical accuracy is not its object. Its purpose is to emphasise and develop the differences which are conceived to be important and to reproduce in all orders behaviour reactions hitherto largely the domain of an exclusive and dominant group. It was not written with the occidental reader in view. This is one of its chief merits. There are, fortunately, many valuable and interesting studies and selected translations now accessible in the English language which have been prepared by eminent Japanese and foreign scholars. For the most part, however, they are special and advanced studies of religious and philosophical schools or movements, political or social histories, analyses of artistic achievements, and biographies, or they are merely curious and topical in their purport. Excellent and important though they may be they have been written with a more or less clear conception of foreign prejudices and literary standards. In order to avoid the pitfalls of distortion and over-emphasis it is necessary to balance such reading with the study of works such as the "Nippon Shindo Ron" written by a Japanese for Japanese and prepared with the avowed intention of dealing only with those difference tendencies upon which the characteristic social and political behaviour of every member of the community is conceived to rest. It is in the hope that this English edition of Mr Hibino's work will serve in part to fulfil this mission, while providing at the same time a source-book for the Meiji period, that the present translation has been undertaken.

In bringing this Introduction to a close the writer wishes to express his hearty appreciation of the invaluable aid which he has received in turn from Mr T. Hara, Rev. K. Fujioka, and Rev. K. Shiraishi. Any merits which the translation may contain are due to their courteous and painstaking assistance.

A. P. McK.

CAMBRIDGE

June 30th, 1928

AUTHOR'S PREFACE

TO THIRD EDITION

WHEN the First Aichi Prefectural Middle School[1] succeeded the Aichi English School many clever and promising youths, who admired its ideals, eagerly sought admission in order that they might develop their innate talents and improve their natural gifts in the most favourable surroundings. For a number of years the reputation of the School steadily increased throughout the whole country. During the decade subsequent to the twentieth year of Meiji (1887), however, it was found impossible to maintain the facilities previously offered at the same high level of excellence. Aspiring scholars at that period suffered disappointment in their search for an institution comparable with this School in its former eminence.[2]

It was at this juncture that a group of my respected seniors and honoured friends urged me to consider that it was my duty to accept the office of principal and endeavour to restore the School to its former position. Though deeply conscious of my own insufficiency for this task I at length consented to entertain their proposal. Mr Gijin Okuda, who was at that time Vice-Minister of Education, and Mr Morikata Oki, the Governor of Aichi Prefecture, united in recommending me for this high honour. I received my official appointment as Principal of the School and took up my duties on the twenty-first day of July in the thirty-second year of Meiji (1899). The impulse to undertake this difficult task was not due solely to the recommendations of my friends. I too realised the true situation and felt that I could not refuse to go to the aid of my home Province. I therefore set

[1] The senior Middle School of Aichi Prefecture. The middle school is designed to give a well-balanced general education to youths between the ages of twelve and eighteen. In general it corresponds to the German gymnasium or more loosely to the secondary school in England or the high school of North America.

[2] A slight condensation in the English version has been approved by the author.

to work at once, though profoundly conscious of my own short-comings, to revise the character of the School and to direct the energies of the pupils into more profitable channels. I made it a point to emphasise the necessity for a parallel development of mind and body, and endeavoured to implant the idea that this dual culture was essential to the true achievement of our national aims. This programme led naturally to the promotion of athletics and a careful direction of attention to those funda-mental conceptions upon which our national institutions are based. I devoted my twenty years of office to the realisation of these objectives, and, although only too conscious of my own lack of ability, endeavoured to direct my personal life in a manner consonant with this purpose. In adopting this course I felt that I was best serving the interests of my home Province and of the Empire at large. Throughout the past twenty years the graduates of this School have risen to positions of eminence, due, I believe, to the balanced vigour of character achieved by this system of instruction. During this period the School be-came widely known for its athletic prowess and the name " Itchu Boy "[1] became a coveted possession. I feel deeply conscious of the fact that the measure of success achieved is due solely to the unfailing sympathy and support which I have received from my many friends. I can never forget the debt which I owe to them.

The chronicles of the past show how our national life is derived from the august condescension of those Sons of Heaven who became our Rulers. The glorious and unique relation of the subject to his Lord has existed unchanged from the earliest times. Consequently on the occasion of the auspicious nuptials of the present Emperor I made bold to publish my first thesis. In it I endeavoured to point out the need for revising our conception of the teachings of morals and ethics. These concep-tions which have emerged from the general welter of world-wide human relations are not adequate to convey the true nature of our unique national life. The incomparable relation

[1] Literally, "First Middle Boy," a student or graduate of the First Pre-fectural Middle School.

of vassal and Lord which is the peculiar possession of this people requires a special term to describe it. I have therefore coined the pregnant phrase "Nippon Shindo"[1] in an attempt to unite in one term those vital and unique conceptions and ideals upon which this Empire is founded, by reason of which it has maintained its separate entity down through the ages and through which it has achieved the proud position it occupies to-day. In this book, which I have entitled "Nippon Shindo Ron," I have endeavoured to set forth in detail all those conceptions which united form our national heritage. Subsequently I re-published this work in the form of a textbook for use in Middle Schools. The Department of Education received the volume kindly and authorised its use as a textbook. Since that time it has been employed as a regular textbook in the First Aichi Prefectural Middle School. The book, "Nippon Shindo Ron," is designed to make clear the central conception upon which our national life is founded. In it I have laid bare my deepest convictions as to the true relation of the subject to his Emperor. For twenty years I have endeavoured to plant these conceptions firmly in the hearts and minds of the scholars entrusted to my care.

I reverently acknowledge the favourable reception of my book within the sacred precincts of the Imperial Palace. I wish also to express my gratitude for its reception by His Excellency Lieutenant-General Haruno Okubo. I deeply appreciate General Okubo's encouragement and his recommendation of my book to the notice of His Excellency General Maresuke Nogi.[2] I wish especially to express my gratitude to General

[1] Literally translated this term means "The Way of the Japanese Subject." The term is noteworthy in that it stands for an important adaptation of Confucian teaching to the requirements of the Japanese national ideals. In the effort to provide the youth of modern Japan with a consistent ethical background Mr Hibino has boldly cut the Gordian knot of the old controversy between loyalty and filial piety. The importance of his contribution is gaining increasing recognition in his own country, and it is on this account that General Nogi referred to him as sensei or teacher.

[2] General Maresuke Nogi, commander of the Third Army in the Russo-Japanese War, hero of Port Arthur, commander of the victorious left wing in the Battle of Mukden, a samurai of the old school and the idol of the Japanese people.

Nogi for reading the whole book through with painstaking care, for the comments he deigned to inscribe in the margin, and for his criticism. I desire to acknowledge also the kindness of General Okubo in obtaining permission for me to make use of these comments which the Commander-in-Chief had written with his own hand, as well as the privilege of inserting at the beginning of this book facsimiles of the original correspondence concerning my work which passed between General Okubo and General Nogi.

When I think of the care with which the Commander-in-Chief himself read and pondered each phrase and sentence I am overwhelmed with a sense of my own unworthiness and with a consciousness of the obvious defects of the book. My sole source of comfort is in the reflection that it may serve to perpetuate the memory of the lofty character and superlative qualities of our great Commander.

By the publication of this book, with the facsimiles of his honoured comments, I hope to make plain to the people at large the anxious thought which this great man devoted to the question of the cultivation of the national spirit, and to the task of arousing and awakening his fellow-countrymen. I am only too conscious of the unsufficiency and inferiority of this discussion. Nevertheless, if my readers are stimulated to a true recognition of that nobility of character which characterised the late General Nogi, and if they are able, at the same time, to realise the sincerity of the motives which have prompted me to publish this book, then there is some possibility of my being able to repay in small part the honour he has done me.

Finally, at the time of General Nogi's death the Editor of the "Yorozu Chōhō," Mr Shuroku Kuroiwa, published in his paper an editorial essay entitled "On hearing of the Devotional Self-Immolation of General Nogi." I take this opportunity of expressing my thanks for his permission to include this essay.

YUTAKA HIBINO

Sixth month of the ninth year of Taishō
(1920)

"ON HEARING OF THE DEVOTIONAL SELF-IMMOLATION OF GENERAL NOGI"

by

SHUROKU KUROIWA

WHETHER the nation has suffered a great loss in the death of General Nogi, or whether, on the other hand, it has been greatly enriched by his death, is the question which we, and more especially the educators of the country, must settle.[1] We must clearly grasp the significance of this question. I consider that we have been brought face to face with the necessity of determining the relation which exists between the responsibilities of loyalty on the one hand and the duties of the individual to himself on the other. In a word, it is a question whether General Nogi by refraining from his sacrifice would have best served the cause of loyalty, or whether by his continued existence he would have served this cause less well.

It is evident that he destroyed himself in order to be united in death to the former Emperor. At the same time it is equally clear that such devotional self-sacrifice is now forbidden in this country.[2] We know also that General Nogi was the recipient of important commands from the late Emperor. It is evident that by his death he avoided the obligations of these commands. One of his duties was the instruction of the sons of the nobility. Further, as a warrior it was his duty to guard and protect the State. In this sense it is clear that he had been entrusted with important duties by the late Emperor.

[1] General Nogi died by his own hand in accordance with the old samurai tradition, at eight o'clock on the evening of September 13th, 1912, this being the hour of the Imperial funeral, which took place, according to custom, on the forty-fifth day after the death of the Emperor. At the time of his death General Nogi was sixty-three years of age.

[2] Junshi, or the custom of self-destruction upon the death of master or mistress, was officially abandoned at a very early date. Some authorities put it as early as the beginning of the Christian era. The Legacy of Ieyasu distinctly prohibits it. The whole of Chapter LXXV of this remarkable document is devoted to a discussion of the subject.

At the same time it is pointed out that his death had in it no element of necessity. He took his life of his own free will and choice.

Do the present-day conceptions of education adjudge his motives correct or otherwise? Let us take the comments of our modern educators on the death of Nankō,[1] who also died by his own hand whilst fighting the Emperor's battles. They contend that Nankō had not determined upon self-immolation from the beginning. It was only as a result of actual conflict when he discovered that his arms and supplies were insufficient for the task entrusted to him by the Emperor that he decided upon death. Nay, they go farther and declare that if he had planned self-immolation from the first as the only means of demonstrating his loyalty when faced with certain failure, if he had determined upon death from the beginning because he anticipated non-adoption of his strategy, if for such reasons as this he took his life in the midst of the conflict, then they contend that his loyalty was imperfect, that there was, in fact, something lacking in it.

This explanation is quite inadmissible in my view. Although it is not my purpose to discuss the problem of Nankō a consideration of the points of similarity between his case and that of General Nogi is illuminating. There are, of course, many historical difficulties in the way of a complete understanding of the situation which gave rise to Nankō's death. Nevertheless, if we consider the facts as we know them reasonably and dispassionately it will appear extremely probable that he had decided upon self-immolation before going into battle. Let us consider this to be the case, for the sake of argument. I must say that I consider his death under these circumstances to be a noble and meritorious act. He was a man of rock-like determination and self-confidence, and it was due to these

---

[1] Otherwise known as Kusunoki Masashige, one of the greatest of Japan's warlike heroes, a pattern of the perfect knight, and champion of the Southern Court. He died by his own hand on July 4th, 1336, when it became apparent that his forlorn hope could no longer hold out against the immensely superior forces of the rebel Takauji.

characteristics that he undertook to defend the isolated strong-hold of Chihaya in the midst of his enemies. Even when he was nearly overwhelmed by Takauji and his rebels at Minatogawa his self-confidence was such that he still conceived that there was another method to be tried. Yet he knew that there were many obstacles to his plan when he had first proposed it at court. In view of the fact that it was not only probable that his plans could not succeed but that there was no way even for a possibility of realisation it is contended that Nankō, of his own free will and on his own responsibility, had determined upon death. He purposely led a small band of warriors to meet the enemy at Minatogawa. He saw clearly that he could not escape defeat and he did not wish to have his followers needlessly slaughtered, therefore he contented himself with a mere handful of retainers. Furthermore, when he was about to set out on this expedition he called his son Masatsura to his side and con-fided his last wishes to him. He pointed out to his son the course which he wished him to follow on reaching man's estate. At this time it may be said that the heart of Nankō displayed a purity of motive the like of which has not been witnessed from ancient times down to the present. Nankō considered that if he were to die in such circumstances people would come to regard his death as an example of loyalty and others would be influenced to give their lives for their country. He felt sure that his own clan at least would not neglect his aspirations. He believed that his death at this juncture would provide a nobler pattern to succeeding generations than his continued existence possibly could. With such thoughts in his mind he faced a battlefield which held inevitable death in store for him, and fought with all his energy until the cause was lost. He left behind a model of how a knight should die. In a physical and material sense he failed and yet in a spiritual sense he succeeded. He well knew that he could not be victorious and he considered that a spiritual victory was in any case of greater importance to the cause.

It is for these reasons that the Southern Dynasty never forgot his noble act. It is for this reason that the memory of his knightly deed is passed on from father to son as a precious treasure. Upheld by the power of this beautiful deed alone the Southern Court, which had neither physical nor material strength, was able to hold out for fifty years. Indeed from that time until the Meiji era five hundred years later, and even down to the Russo-Japanese War, a multitude of followers has arisen which has striven to emulate the glorious example of Nankō. This deed has gone far to nourish among the sons of Yamato that flower of loyalty and courage which has so astonished the world. The spirit of Nankō who determined upon death as the highest expression of his loyalty has influenced the hearts of our people in the past and will continue to do so as long as this country shall stand. The memory of his deed will never be lost.

I hold, therefore, that Nankō demonstrates his greatness in the preparation he made for death, and in the deliberate choice which he made of the noble way which led to self-immolation. When I take this stand it is a foregone conclusion that I should be dissatisfied with the explanations of our present-day educators.

Men are endowed with individual responsibilities. They must determine not only whether it is their duty to live or to die but all other questions as well. In view of this responsibility there sometimes—nay, often—arise situations in which the individual duties seem to conflict with the claims of the nation. The country to-day does not recognise the possibility of such variation. It would force each individual into the same mould and prohibit the free development of his personality, his free thinking and acting. The country seems bent on developing those characteristics which make for facile leading and direction. Even the principles of education have been altered to suit the present fondness for uniformity. It is not surprising, therefore, that we find our educators explaining that Nankō had not decided on self-immolation from the first, for if he had there would have been some defect in his otherwise perfect loyalty. In other words they construct a hypothesis which is contrary to the commonsense of mankind. They even construe historical facts in a way that will not fit the reality. They try to make out that the individual rights and freedoms which are the very essence of individual responsibility are in themselves evil things. This state of affairs has persisted until the present day. Now we have a right to ask how they are going to regard the death of General Nogi. Unless they now declare that General Nogi was not a truly loyal person they only manifest the falsity of their own position.

I hold that we must regard General Nogi and Nankō in the same light. On his own responsibility and from a deep sense of a higher duty General Nogi disposed of his life. Nevertheless, what General Nogi considered to be the best course seems to conflict with what the nation considers to be the correct procedure. Will the people, therefore, acknowledge this deed or will they denounce it? If they denounce it they will by that act perpetuate and sustain the wilful falsity which is now inherent in our educational ideals. If, on the other hand, the nation as a whole acknowledges and lauds this act their attitude will coincide exactly with the point of view which I daily advocate in the columns of the press.

I consider General Nogi to be the greatest hero, since Nankō, that our nation has produced. He is more demigod than man. He led the great assault on Port Arthur. He sacrificed his own son by placing him in positions of greatest difficulty and danger. Having lost one son he sent the other into identical dangers and lost him also. It was not that he did not love his sons. Because he sent countless brothers and children of others to death on the battlefield he could not discriminate in favour of his own flesh and blood. Urged on by a deep sense of moral responsibility, influenced by the noblest and most lofty considerations, and suffering keenly as he did for the bereaved families of the fallen, he had no other course than to sacrifice his sons. As the popular poem puts it:

It is unworthy to weep for an only son when there is one who has lost two.

As General Nogi has lost his two sons, those who have lost but one son upon the field of battle cannot grieve with him.

On the conclusion of the Russo-Japanese War he returned covered with glory in company with the other heroes of that conflict. He alone cherished a sorrowing heart in the midst of the nation's welcome. He felt that he had nothing adequate to say to the bereaved relatives of the fallen and would hardly look anyone in the face. Where can we find his equal for beauty of character? In ancient times General Kōu of the country of So, while still on the eastern side of the river, destroyed himself as a mark of his grief at the loss of so many young men. Not only is this one of the beautiful deeds of Chinese tradition, it is one which is worthy of being recorded as a world-wide example. It is only just that our people should praise this ancient Chinese hero and regard him as a pattern of chivalry. General Nogi's deed, however, has a greater merit—Kōu returned in defeat, but General Nogi returned in glorious victory and the renown of great deeds successfully accomplished. Since his return his deeds and thoughts have suffered no diminution in greatness or nobility. Who can refrain from praising him? He has now joined his Emperor in death. By such a death he has maintained the exalted nobility of his former conduct. In his death he has exhibited the purest of loyalty. Does anyone suppose that he was not aware that by this act he cast aside the soldier's duty of guarding his country and his duty as an educator of the sons of the nobility? The thought of these very duties was an added incentive to his deed. It was because General Nogi was General Nogi that he could perform this act, to which none other could attain. He determined on death as Nankō did before him. He sorrowed deeply when he saw a people attracted by the superficial glamour of great acts of loyalty yet lacking utterly a conception of the spiritual grounds from which they spring. He desired by his death to clarify our vision. He died to save men from this wave of superficiality. By his loyal and patriotic act he desired to prevent empty and slavish subservience to mere formalities. He realised that his own devotional death was the only way by which he could leave behind a strong and effective spiritual influence which would be potent to release the nation from these errors. For these reasons I contend that nothing could have been more necessary or more beautiful than his death. He was convinced that his death was befitting the spirit of a warrior and more beneficial to the youth of the nation than his continued existence as an educator. His devotional self-immolation has power to rescue our nation from degenerate tendencies and will never cease to be a powerful influence for good.

His self-immolation and the fact that his wife immediately followed his example indicate a rare purity of character displayed in the home life. Individuals who are unable to influence the characters of those who come into closest contact with them are truly unable to influence others. Those whose home life is unhappy can do little to increase the happiness of society. Those, however, who manifest elements of sublimity in their home life are really great. On the other hand those who do not observe the traditional virtues of the home are not worthy of respect. Those who cannot direct their own households by the influence of their characters are unable to influence others for good. General Nogi's character, however, had a profound influence on the lives both of his sons and of his wife. Those who were closest to him were most influenced by his spirit, and joyfully sought with him to offer their lives for their country. What a profound influence this deed will have for thousands, nay, tens of thousands of years upon the people of our country! How hopeless is the condition of this country if it fails to be influenced by this lofty deed! What an opportunity his death affords for arousing those who seem impervious to all spiritual appeal! None are so degenerate as to be beyond the influence of his glorious death. I offer him the sincerest gratitude of my heart. Nevertheless, though I offer my gratitude I am at the same time only too conscious of my own unworthiness. My only desire is to be stimulated to worthier living by his example. Though I am utterly inadequate for the task I yet desire to offer this poor token of my gratitude.

I know not how this nation can ever repay its debt to him nor
how we can acceptably transmit the nobility of his character
to our descendants, nor do I know how this country, on account
of contrary views held in some quarters, can ever do anything
effective to express its appreciation of his great qualities.
And yet I believe that the people must of necessity do something
to commemorate this deed. Shall we accord him reverence as
a demigod? If we cannot so regard him then whom indeed can
we regard in this light? Nevertheless, whether we so revere him
and so acknowledge him or not he is indeed already a demigod
—more than man. Those who would acknowledge his heroic
qualities and refuse to render him the reverence which is his due
are altogether ignorant of what is right and proper. It is not
necessary to search further in the annals of history to discover
examples of heroic, lofty, and beautiful character. In him we
find true heroism, true nobility, and true beauty. By merely
living in this age we are privileged to live with demigods. No
man could be more godlike than he. Unless we deify and
worship him in our hearts we cannot have the perpetual privilege
and joy of fellowship with him. Truly General Nogi was more
than mortal man.

> Till this day we thought him a hero
> Now he seems a god born among men.

CORRESPONDENCE, WITH FACSIMILES

Letter of MR KUROIWA *to* MR HIBINO

In reply to your communication with regard to the article "On Hearing of the Devotional Self-Immolation of General Nogi", I consider it an honour that it should be included in your book "Nippon Shindo Ron" and hereby consent to its insertion.

SHUROKU KUROIWA

To MR YUTAKA HIBINO

Facsimile of Letter of GENERAL NOGI *to* GENERAL OKUBO[1]

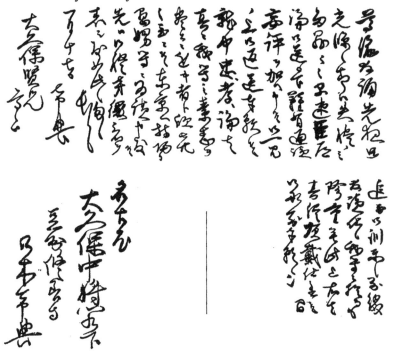

[1] In the translation formal salutations and addresses have been abridged and all names given in the usual English order. Otherwise the letters have been rendered into English as written.

The facsimiles have been reduced to about one-fourth original size in order to facilitate inclusion in the English text.

(*Translation.*) With respect to your communication which I received last night, I may say that I have read with pleasure the book "Shindo Ron" which you sent me. I have added a few notes and comments to the text. After looking through it will you kindly return it to me. It gives me pleasure to note that the conception of loyalty and filial piety insisted upon very nearly coincides with what I have always held. I have therefore perused the sentiments of this book with pleasure.

I shall take it back to Tokyo with me and shall instruct my nephews to read it. In conclusion, please accept my sincere thanks.

Hastily,

MARESUKE NOGI

To GENERAL HARUNO OKUBO

P.S. I have read the further note to which you called my attention. I consider that nothing is of greater importance to us than this. I should like to inform you that I accept it as it is.

M. N.

Facsimile of Letter of GENERAL OKUBO *to* MR HIBINO

(*Translation.*) I am glad to hear that you are all enjoying good health. With regard to the copy of "Nippon Shindo Ron" which you sent me I have shown it to General Nogi. He returned it to me last night with valuable notes attached.

While at Shuzenji he has devoted three or four days to the perusal of the book. Although these comments are not the result of lengthy consideration and study they are still evidences of his opinions and of the fact that he has devoted earnest study to this subject.

I forward the copy for your information and beg you to return it as soon as you have perused it. I shall postpone further comment until we meet.

HARUNO OKUBO

To MR YUTAKA HIBINO

P.S. I enclose also General Nogi's letter which I beg you to return as soon as you have read it.

H. O.

Facsimile of Letter of GENERAL NOGI *to* GENERAL OKUBO

(*Translation.*) I am glad to hear that you are enjoying good health. With regard to the copy of "Shindo Ron" which you sent me recently, I should like to say that I intended my insignificant notes solely for your private perusal.

I am rather put out that you forwarded them at once to Mr Hibino ("Hibino Sensei").[1] If I had known that such was your intention I should have written more carefully. However, it cannot be helped now. In the future I shall be more careful.

On second thought I am inclined to regard the rough expression of opinion which I have inscribed in this copy of the book as a joke at my expense.

Although I expected you would return the original you have gone to the trouble of sending me a new copy. I am sorry to cause you so much inconvenience. Please accept my sincere thanks. When we meet I shall take pleasure in telling you more than I can in the limits of this short note.

Hastily,

MARESUKE NOGI

To GENERAL HARUNO OKUBO

   THE NAGOYA GARRISON

      HIS EXCELLENCY LIEUT.-GENERAL OKUBO,

Private Correspondence.

TOKYO, AKASAKA,

   MARESUKE NOGI.

Facsimile of Letter of GENERAL OKUBO *to* MR HIBINO

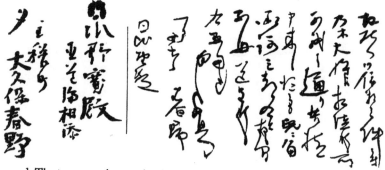

---

[1] The term sensei or teacher has special connotations among the Japanese. It is an honourable term and its use in this context by General Nogi is highly complimentary to the author.

(*Translation.*) In regard to your request I have consulted General Nogi. As you see by the enclosure, although he demurs, he at least consents to the proposal. I am therefore sending another copy of the book to him.

HARUNO OKUBO

To MR YUTAKA HIBINO

AUTHOR'S PREFACE

TO FIRST EDITION

DIVINE providence has placed human beings upon the earth and has accorded them rules for the regulation of their lives. Nations have been formed and laws divinely granted for the conduct of their affairs. By the observance of these rules and these laws each member of the state may achieve the full development of his natural gifts and maintain the integrity of his character. To do this is the divinely appointed task of each individual. There is as wide a diversity in men's abilities as in their features. Men differ in character as well as in deeds. Nor are they equal in moral capacity or material possessions.

Although there are many nations upon the surface of the earth yet their relations with one another resemble the mutual relations of individuals in a state.

The aggregation of human beings forms society, a group of families the clan. Penalties are also established for the restraint of society and for the control of the clan. Although there are standards of moral conduct for the individual, for the nation, for the state, for society, and for the clan, nevertheless the foundations of morality are found either in the idea of righteousness or in some theory of the highest good.

In their endeavour to realise such moral ideals some place the emphasis upon natural laws, some upon man-made regulations. Some place one above the other, others would collect all laws together and make an eclectic choice. Although the sphere of morals is boundless and without limit nevertheless the aim is the realisation of good in the individual life, the cultivation of a true national spirit, and the happiness and well-being of society at large. In publishing this book " Nippon Shindo Ron " I am well aware of the fact and gladly acknowledge that this Empire which stands for ever at the gate of Asia extends the hand of cordial fellowship to other nations, while striving at the same time to increase the happiness and prosperity of its own people. It is not my intention to enforce a narrow, in-dividualistic conception of morals. It is simply my desire that we Japanese shall as citizens of Japan serve this most noble of Empires and our Emperor with hearts of true loyalty and patriotism. This book is but the expression of my most earnest hope that they may learn how to realise this lofty ideal. I have no other desire above this.

I have summed up this ideal in the words "Nippon Shindo". Nippon Shindo is the true Way by which each subject of the Emperor is enabled to fulfil all his obligations with whole-hearted devotion. By such fulfilment the national glory will increase with each passing day, and the national prestige will be enhanced with each successive month. Keeping this ideal ever firmly in mind we must seek to learn the sacred will of the Emperor. This is indeed the dearest wish and the highest endeavour of every subject. With these words I bring this Preface to a close.

YUTAKA HIBINO

Sixth month of the thirty-seventh year of Meiji
   (1904)

INTRODUCTORY

WHAT is the present condition of society in this country?
Is public morality widely practised or does evil
flourish? I do not propose to concern myself chiefly
with criticism or discussion of opinions of this nature, neverthe-.
less, I cannot fail to note that many, observing the trend of
modern society, heap abuse upon it and call it degenerate, while
seeming to pride themselves upon their own purity. Is society
advancing towards decay with the passage of time? Are there
tendencies which hinder the development of those virtues upon
which depend the health and well-being of the social organisation? The natural complexity of two thousand five hundred
years of living history renders difficult the task of offering an
immediate answer to these questions. There are, of course,
many organisations like the Temperance Society or the Women's
Friendly Societies which work continually and whole-heartedly
to improve the condition of society, to develop character, and
to encourage the practice of the beautiful customs of the past.
The question whether these movements are simply ephemeral
reactions or whether they are the true products and developments of the age is not an easy one to determine. In general
there exist in society means of promoting moral ideals, enforcing
right conduct, and cultivating noble qualities. Consideration of
such facts should effectually silence these lamentations and
complaints regarding degeneracy. So long as these means are
effectively employed then no matter how great or how complex
the problems there need be no fear that noble ideals will be
neglected or the five virtues disregarded. Let us direct our
attention, however, to the practices of those who teach ethics
and morals to-day. I fear that there are few indeed who adopt
the correct measures and the appropriate means of influencing
society and educating men in the sphere of morals. This situation is a constant source of anxiety. Those who have a true
interest in such problems can never suffer them to be neglected.

Nevertheless, they are for the most part so difficult and complicated that solutions are hard to find.

Moral teachings are the pillars and foundations of society. They are the bed-rock of national virtue. Without them neither society nor state could exist for a single day. If there are defects in these teachings society is to that extent rendered susceptible to harm. It will be seen, therefore, that morality is truly a weighty matter. It is to be regretted that there are so few who comprehend the inner aspect of morality. How few there are who know how to navigate this boundless ocean! I cannot help but feel that if those who ignorantly and superficially bewail the decline of manners and the unpopularity of virtuous ideals would lay their scorn aside and bestir themselves "to plant the hemp in preparation for the braiding of the rope", in other words if they would engage in a positive and constructive course of action, some good would be accomplished. Our Government, realising the importance of taking action, has already established the Society for the Discussion of Ethical Principles. This Society carries on an investigation of ethical principles and teachings which is of the utmost service in popularising this necessary discipline. Such valuable measures are especially opportune at this time. I sincerely hope that they will succeed.

Unfortunately, most of those who attempt to teach ethics cherish the vain hope that we Japanese can successfully undertake to live in accordance with some foreign system of ethics—what has been called "Asiatic" ethics for example, or even "universal" ethics. This arises from the idea of the solidarity of the race. We can, unhappily, see only too clearly on all sides the effect of these ill-considered and confused ideas. This situation should not be allowed to continue for a single day. With the Restoration[1] foreign civilisation flooded our country and the concrete elements of our own culture as well as the abstract underwent various changes. The people unwisely accepted the offerings of the four seas without sufficient

---

[1] The Restoration of Imperial rule and the overthrow of the Tokugawa Shogunate. The date is that of the accession of the Emperor Meiji, 1868.

discrimination. This is an evil which was perhaps inevitable under the circumstances and should not be too severely censured. Nevertheless, it was an unprofitable situation and one which far-seeing men regretted exceedingly. Shall our country, placed as it is among the nations like a piece on a chess board, direct the lives of its citizens by systems of ethics eastern or western or even that system which is called "universal"? It seems to me that there is no question as to whether the people of Japan should observe either a foreign, an eastern, or a universal system of ethics. We have our own peculiar system of ethics. We possess already a system which is adapted to the Japanese people. I cannot help feeling that Nippon Shindo, the Way of the Japanese Subject, is the most suitable system for this people. As the Way which Japanese people should naturally follow and the duties which they must observe are one and the same, let us set aside the words "Rinri" (ethical principles) and "Shushin" (moral culture) and recommend the term "Shindo" which coincides so much better with our national aspirations and characteristics. Shindo epitomises in one term all the loftiest aspirations of our compatriots.

What Way·is this that every individual subject must aspire to observe? The Way, which from the dawn of our history has been the chief object of our aspirations, the object towards which all our tendencies and habits point, the Way which each subject must follow is nothing less than loyalty itself. Other than loyalty there is no way for the Japanese subject to follow. It is loyalty that guards and maintains the immutable permanence of the Imperial Dynasty. It is the source from which spring sentiments of true love for the Emperor and true patriotism for the country. Loyalty is the very life and spinal nerve of the Japanese subject. It is my firm conviction that the ethical principles of the Japanese people must be based upon the unique foundation of loyalty. The mutual obligations of children and parents, of relatives, of husband and wife, the duties of friendship and human brotherhood are all practical means for manifesting, accomplishing, and fulfilling the central obligation of loyalty.

With loyalty as the stem the branches of filial piety, fraternal spirit, tranquillity in the home, trust in friends all take their natural order. It is in this sense that these virtues should be cultivated and encouraged. In this manner alone can the Japanese subject completely observe and fulfil the obligations of the Way. For the Japanese subject loyalty is indeed the unique and original source of all ethical culture as well as the impulse of all true deeds. Every ethical act is included and implied in that unique noun "Shindo". All the inner meanings of the word loyalty are included in the wider sense in which this term is used.

I should like to consider at this juncture some of the traditional precepts of loyalty and filial piety which we hold in such reverence. I consider that the well-known saying, namely, "The loyal subject issues from the home where filial piety is revered" should be reversed. It should be, "The filial son is found in the home where loyalty is revered". The teaching that "the higher duty casts parents aside" should rather be that when confronted by the higher duty of loyalty the lesser duty to parents ceases to exist. In other words, the teaching that filial piety is the source of all virtue must be altered by substituting loyalty for filial piety. When claiming that loyalty is the single Way we do not deny the obligations of filial piety. We simply regard filial piety as one of the manifestations of loyalty. Loyalty is indeed our highest good and all virtuous action originates therein. Let us hereafter abandon the contention that there is a universal set of ethical principles in the world. I believe that there are different sets of ethical principles peculiar to orient and occident. I believe further that there is a special set of ethical principles applicable only to Japan. There already exists in this country the teaching of Shindo which is naturally suited to the genius of the Japanese people.

To conclude my argument, I propose to call by the name of "Shindo" what has hitherto been known as "teachings regarding ethical principles". I propose also to make many variations in the original teachings of ethical principles. I shall

make loyalty the basic principle of Shindo in order that the title
and the reality may accord well. By this means I hope to improve
the culture of our country and permanently to elevate the character
of our people. Such measures are of the utmost importance in
the present chaotic state of civilisation. Therefore, I have considered this to be an opportune time for urging upon all the
adoption of the teachings of Shindo. It is commonly held that
the repudiation of fundamental obligations results in the decay
of morality. Indeed, the cultivation of these virtues is as
necessary to human life as the elements of fire and water. It
is not for me to discuss, however, whether universal obligations
or moral conduct suffer decline in the manner popularly held.
I think it is of greater moment to proceed at once to the study
of the fundamental conceptions of Shindo, to make plain the
source of these doctrines, and to establish the authority of this
conception in human affairs. I firmly believe that we must
devote all our energy to seeking a permanent means of enforcing
these teachings. I have already referred to the elements of
Shindo, and the Japanese people are acquainted with the main
outlines of the teachings included under this head. It may seem
unnecessary, therefore, for me to express my humble opinions
regarding Shindo. Nevertheless, I believe that it is worth while
stating my point of view and making a practical appeal to the
intelligence of the educated classes. By means of their helpful
criticism I hope that the doctrine may be still further developed.
My only desire is to do what little I can to enhance the prosperity
and well-being of my country.

If it is asked what Shindo is a single word suffices for answer,
namely, loyalty. If it is then asked what loyalty is and what it
implies we reply briefly that it means the unchanging reverential
service of the Imperial Line. Blossoming into expression it is
the beauty and fragrance of a myriad cherry flowers, hoarded
it is the beauty of a hundred tempered blades. Its beauty is
manifest in the heroic death of Nankō and in the words of
Shigemori's reproof. For all the glorious deeds of the past,
unparalleled in the annals of the east or west, there is but one

explanation, namely, loyalty. There can be no doubt whatever regarding the truth of this assertion. Though the world is wide and humanity past numbering these deeds of loyalty are the peculiar pride and possession of this nation. They constitute the special virtue and significance of our national flag. There can be no Shindo without loyalty. Loyalty is the central pillar of the state, and the very life of the Japanese subject. To this proposition I firmly believe there is not one dissenting voice among the myriad subjects of the Empire. When it comes to the question of cultivating, advancing, and practising this loyalty which is solely the possession of the Japanese nation and the essential element in Shindo I regret exceedingly that my own ideals and the present tendencies are radically opposed. I cannot remain silent in the face of this situation. My anxiety is increased because these tendencies reflect upon the doctrine of Shindo. I have already explained that Shindo is loyalty. Loyalty is that privilege accorded to the subject by means of which he may for ever manifest true service to the throne. From this explanation and this definition it will be clear wherein I differ in my opinions from the position popularly held at present. In taking this position I feel constrained to offer my apologies to my seniors and humbly anticipate their correction. If I were to express my opinions in order I should arrange them as follows:

    I. Regulations which govern the Imperial Household.
    II. The National Constitution.
    III. The Imperial Rescript.

Shindo, ethical principles, and moral culture all take their rise in these three sources. I must explain why I consider my opinions to be valid. My third reference is, of course, to the Rescript on Education,[1] which I shall hereafter simply call the Rescript.

---

[1] The Imperial Rescript on Education (Chokugo) was first promulgated on October 30th, 1890. It is always read in the schools at the beginning of the year, on the occasion of the Imperial birthday, and at other important anniversaries or ceremonies. It has undoubtedly had a profound effect in shaping the thought of modern Japan.

To serve the Emperor with single-hearted loyalty and to sacrifice one's self courageously for the public good, are the natural duties of the Japanese subject. They remain unaltered by the passage of time. They are the superlative treasures of the Japanese subject by reason of which he rises superior to all foreign peoples. We should treasure these noble characteristics. They are not to be abandoned even should the waters of the Kamogawa flow backward in their bed. My only anxiety is lest those who endeavour to serve the Emperor with loyalty and the state with devotion, and who direct others in this service, should themselves be ignorant of the true source of all authority and of the Regulations which refer to the Imperial Succession. Should they remain in ignorance of these things then, in times of national disturbances which cover the sky like a cloud and the earth with blood, loyal subjects though desiring to serve out of pure and honest hearts may yet be unable to discover where their true duty lies. There is therefore a great danger that their services may be lost to the state, and that they may die in vain.

In order to allay these anxieties all subjects must be taught the objects towards which their loyalty should be directed, and the sphere in which they should display their virtuous conduct. They must also be taught that loyalty is the true expression of reverence to the Imperial House. And they must further be instructed with care in what manner the Regulations governing the Imperial Household are applied.

Merely to urge the observance of loyalty without a knowledge of the Regulations governing the Imperial Household is an extremely dangerous proceeding. There is a danger that such leading may result in useless and empty expressions of loyalty and courage. While teaching the reasons for observing the doctrine of loyalty it is the natural order to draw attention first to the true object of loyalty. In the second place the subject must be taught how this Imperial Household, which is the object of his loyalty, is itself governed. This, it seems to me, is the obvious order and the necessary division of the subject.

Nevertheless, when we examine the teachings of those who discourse on ethical principles and lecture on morals we find that few indeed have anything to say about the Regulations which govern the Imperial Household. I cannot help regarding this as one of the faults of the times. It is manifested, too, most clearly in educational circles.

The Constitution embodies the great principles upon which the nation is established. It is the source of authority and power and it makes plain the Regulations which govern the lives of subjects. As Japanese subjects who desire to fulfil the demands of loyalty we must be acquainted with the articles of this Constitution. To endeavour to be loyal and virtuous without an acquaintance with this Constitution, which is the basic law of the land, is like looking for fish up a tree. Those who do not understand the Constitution may have hearts full of true patriotism and yet may find themselves unable to display this virtue to advantage. Such persons are liable to stumble into infractions of the Imperial commands out of ignorance. They may thus fail to reciprocate the august grace of our Ruler. Therefore, Japanese subjects who desire to fulfil their natural duties cannot afford to remain in ignorance of the Constitution of their own country. Nevertheless, when we examine the teachings of those who discourse on ethics and lecture on moral culture we find few indeed who have anything to say about the Constitution of this Empire. This, again, is a shortcoming particularly evident among the ranks of our educators.

The Imperial Rescript graciously vouchsafed to us on the thirtieth day of the tenth month of the twenty-third year of Meiji (1890), and known popularly as the Imperial Rescript on Education, teaches the subject how to live in accordance with ethical principles. Its importance lies in the fact that, in accordance with the Regulations which govern the Imperial Household, it inculcates reverence for the Imperial Family, and in accordance with the articles of the Constitution, it enforces the duty of obedience to the Emperor. I humbly venture to suggest that the august heart of our Emperor expects that there will be no misapprehensions in the fulfilment of their duties on the part of his subjects, the flower and pride of his Empire. Unless I am greatly mistaken, it teaches us clearly how to exalt the Imperial Line, how to obey the Imperial commands, and in fact, how we ought to live in this land of Japan. It is important for us to realise that the Regulations which govern the Imperial Household and the Constitution both stand behind the Imperial Rescript. Unfortunately, however, those who teach ethical principles and lecture on morals concentrate their attention upon the Rescript and overlook the vital importance of the Regulations governing the Imperial Household and the Constitution of the country. Is not this an example of foolish neglect? This is one of the faults of the times to which educators are peculiarly prone. This is a fault of our modern textbooks on ethics and morals which we cannot pass over in silence.

The Japanese people are placed in the midst of other nations and have constant intercourse with them. It is not our part to stand aloof. On the one hand, as Japanese subjects we observe the teachings of Shindo, on the other hand, as members of the family of nations we should be acquainted with the courtesies and amenities of intercourse with foreigners. I feel sure that all will agree with me here. It is hardly necessary to devote further space to this subject.

In concluding the above argument I should like to point out that the writings on Shindo (usually called writings on the principles of ethics and morals) are commonly divided into two parts, an internal or national section and an external or international section. In the first section the way each Japanese subject should follow is clearly explained. In the second section there should be a description of the way to be followed in intercourse with foreigners. Again, in the national section, the Laws of the Imperial Household and the Constitution of the state should be fully explained. The Rescript, which embodies the great principles of service to the Imperial Throne, in accordance with the Laws of the Imperial Household, and the Constitution of the state, must then be fully explained and understood. This arrangement of studies based upon the Rescript is the most suitable and convenient one. Most popular writings on morals and ethics have not, up to the present, contained any adequate discussion of these essential subjects. I greatly deplore this state of affairs and venture to publish my own insignificant opinions on these important subjects.

I humbly request the judgement of the intelligentsia on my attempt. I have made bold to publish this book regardless of my own unworthiness. I hope that my indulgent readers will vouchsafe their sympathy and make due allowances.

CHAPTER I

The Empire of Japan

ALTHOUGH from ancient times the area of our Empire has been strictly limited it has never been allowed to grow less through foreign aggression. Everyone admits the limited extent of our domains. In size they are no more than a rifle bullet or a blemish on the skin. Notwithstanding the mere handful of territory occupied by the Empire here on the outer fringe of the Asiatic continent we Japanese are content with the decrees of providence, and not without reason.

History is evidence of the fact that the strong oppress the weak, and that vigorous nations overpower those which are inferior. Living in such a world and familiar with the story of such conditions we are not greatly concerned when we witness the raging seas of worldly power dash high in angry turbulence. We recall the good fortune of our Empire whose integrity has not been injured by the poison fangs and cunning claws of foreign foes. Unharmed and unhindered by enemies the Empire calmly evolves its glorious destiny. The rapid and steady progress of our people is witnessed on every side. Heaven has granted the Empire an Immutable Line and Succession of Emperors who graciously condescend to rule over us. On the other hand generation after generation of loyal vassals has lived with but a single thought, to guard and serve that Throne. From the very dawn of history this Empire has been firmly established and the steady accretions of power and prestige are not a sudden growth but the natural consequences of those fundamental institutions and relations upon which the national life is founded. This is due to the fact that the descendants have ever firmly cherished whatever was revered by their ancestors. Disintegration and separation within the state become impossible when all classes of society co-operate firmly upon these ancient foundations. In this lonely spot, therefore, we find a nation characterised by

beautiful ideals, and possessed of a unique relation between
Emperor and vassal. It is but natural that we should find here
subjects whose conceptions and ideals of loyalty are altogether
unique.

The reasons for the impregnable integrity of the nation and
the unchanging maintenance of our society are beyond reckoning.
The nation, which does not neglect the military arts in time of
peace, is assured a persistent integrity. The parallel cultivation
of the arts of learning and of war will produce a strong and
vigorous state. Over-emphasis of one art to the detriment of
the other must inevitably lead to overthrow and downfall. In
time of peace we must cultivate learning, encourage agriculture,
stimulate commerce, develop the arts and crafts, and endeavour
in every way to increase the wealth and prosperity of the country.
In addition we must never overlook the necessity for the cultivation of military arts and the preparation of our weapons so
that they may be ready for instant use.[1] The prosperity and
power of a nation depend upon a careful adjustment and attention to these details, and the true destiny of the nation cannot
be realised without this discipline.

Cultivation of learning and the military arts must be accompanied by progress in social development. Those who merely
concentrate upon these two arts and pride themselves upon their
accomplishments must not overlook the good points of others
or refuse to make use of their good qualities. Such exclusive
pride will end in disaster. It is simply due to the fact that we
have enjoyed a superior cultivation of the arts of learning and
war that we have been able to maintain the peaceful prosperity
of our country. Vainly to pride ourselves upon our accomplishment and despise others is not a course followed by clear-
sighted and intelligent men. We should not forget that
such clear-sighted vision has much to do with the welfare
of the nation, and the peace and prosperity of our people.
In this connection it will be sufficient to mention the well-

[1] For General Nogi's marginal comments on this passage see Appendix,
paragraph 1.

known examples provided by our Empire, Korea, and China.[1]

There is nothing upon which leaders have looked with such anxiety of late as the torrential violence with which the products of European and American civilisation have invaded the east. The east has literally been flooded with this new civilisation. The foundations of our eastern civilisations have been loosened. Korea leaps forward like a spirited and ungovernable horse. China too has reached a critical point in her development. Although bearing the brunt of this assault our Empire has assimilated the new elements with great success, keeping what is valuable and rejecting the unimportant. We have indeed guided our bark with the utmost care and we therefore now float calmly upon the flood of peaceful development, and are able to direct our course with confidence towards the opposing shore. By means of this new civilisation these orphaned islands of the eastern Asiatic world have prospered and developed. Learning and the arts of war have advanced side by side with the vigour of young and fiery steeds.

A nation's prosperity or its downfall is often equally the result of the penetration of foreign culture. Especially is this the case when the penetration has been excessively rapid. From earliest antiquity down to the present our nation has received but three such contributions, the first from India, the second from China, and the third from Europe and America. All of these accretions have tested the foundations of the nation. We were never dismayed in the midst of these mighty winds and waves but continued to borrow capital from foreign countries and still more to strengthen our already strong position. With every infusion of new ideas our Imperial destiny has been vigorously fostered. The gifts of civilisation are now found in every part of the country. To profit by these contacts and to seize true opportunities when they are presented requires skilful and open-minded leadership. How else could the present prosperity

[1] For General Nogi's marginal comments on this passage see Appendix, paragraph 2.

have been achieved? In the past there are many instances of intercourse with the outer world which have resulted in profit to us. There are, for example, the campaign against Genkō,[1] and more recently the Sino-Japanese and Russo-Japanese Wars.

The progress achieved in this Empire due to the inspiration and influences which have reached us through the channels of foreign intercourse is almost incredible. We have closely inspected these other civilisations and supplemented our own insufficiencies out of their plentiful store. We have taken whatever possessed true value and beauty and enhanced our own possessions by this means. By these contacts and gifts the glory and consequence of our destiny have been fostered by valuable alterations in our national institutions as well as in the domestic sphere of our national life. We have devoted our best energies to these activities in order that we may not fall behind others in the path of progress, or fail to maintain the prosperity of the nation. Those who read history aright are well aware of the importance of these considerations.

Since the Meiji Restoration the influx of western civilisation has been so great that we have scarcely had time to assimilate it. In the midst of this chaos our Empire has steadily and vigorously progressed and has refused to permit its enemies to jeopardise its future. Thus it has achieved its present position of power and prestige. If we consider, for example, the question of legal affairs we find that we are second to none in the details of this important branch of civilisation. The people of this land are well acquainted with the art of ruling and controlling themselves. We have also become skilful in the details of modern

---

[1] The campaign against the Mongol invaders. Kublai Khan's first envoy succeeded in reaching Japan in 1268. The first invading army of 40,000 landed in Kyūshū on November 19th, 1274, met with determined resistance, was overtaken by a great storm, and withdrew in confusion after having sustained a loss of more than 13,000 men. On June 23rd, 1281, the second and greater expedition began to reach the shores of Japan. It is said to have numbered upwards of 100,000 men and 3500 vessels. After some seven weeks of desperate fighting in which the Japanese warriors successfully held the invaders in check another great tornado came to their aid (August 14th and 15th). According to the contemporary records the invading host with its naval equipage was completely annihilated.

business and commerce. Truly the country enjoys abundance and the people multiply. High and low alike enjoy the privileges and amenities of life. Who would not willingly give his life for such a country in the hour of its danger, as a token of gratitude for benefits received.

From ancient times this nation has been rich in a courageous and valiant military spirit, and in a high respect for fidelity and righteousness. The beauty of loyal courage which always shone most brightly in time of danger is something in which we do well to take pride. Wise rule in time of peace, dignified and successful conduct of international business, the establishment of friendly relations with foreign countries and peoples, steady application to the development and advancement of commercial relations, supplying the needs of our own and other countries by the mutual exchange of commodities, these are all practical expressions of the spirit of loyal service.

If foreign nations in their pride of power should venture to despise us, to cause us embarrassment, or to oppress us for their own ends, our Emperor will not overlook their insults, and our people at his command will brave a thousand deaths to defend the national honour. To offer our lives to the Emperor in order that our foes may be defeated and subdued is our highest privilege. These virtues were displayed in the Sino-Japanese War, and more recently in the war with Russia, in which our victorious soldiery has proved its valour sufficiently in a hundred dazzling victories.

Throughout its long history a steady and uninterrupted progress has marked the development of our nation. We glory in the fact that heaven has vouchsafed to us a sacred and immutable Imperial Line. How can the theories and national ideals of foreign countries, whose histories are an unending record of political and social vicissitudes, alternate mutual conquests, and the rise and fall of dynasties, be applied to this Empire whose development and history are utterly unique? The greatness of other nations is as ephemeral as the beauty of the morning glory. Their destinies differ from our own. We do not need the instruction of wise leaders to enforce this contention. Although our country is situated here on the outer fringe of eastern Asia it is nevertheless endowed with a sacred, immutable, and unbroken Line of Emperors, a glorious Succession of Rulers which has existed since time immemorial and which will endure coeval with heaven and earth. Below, the Emperor's faithful subjects and retainers offer their lives in his service, while from above his august and benevolent grace is bestowed in the paternal governance of his devoted vassals. In truth ours is a unique country and a unique people. How glorious is that Empire and how fortunate its subjects!

CHAPTER II

The Japanese Subject

IN order to establish a national organisation three things are necessary, namely, government, subjects, and territory. Should one of these be lacking the national organisation is incomplete. Unless the structure of authority is firmly established among the people, unless there is proper control and just government we have nothing but a land and a people existing side by side and a true nation does not exist. On the other hand even if there should be government and subjects if they possess no territory a true nation cannot exist nor can national institutions develop. Furthermore, even if a people should exist and possess lands if they lack a lawgiver to establish government then again there can be no nation. A true nation requires government, people, and territory, and a national organisation cannot exist when any one of these is lacking. We must realise that government, people, and territory are the three essentials of a national organisation. Once we have grasped the true nature of these three essentials we shall also be able to understand why a country must have its periods of progress and regression, its epochs of power and weakness, its cycles of development and reaction. Although, when we examine the history of a nation, the vicissitudes of its development, its successive rise and fall, its vigour and its weakness, its progress and regression present an innumerable variety of aspects, nevertheless we must admit that the path of true national progress is ever constant. If those who direct the destinies of the nation are instructed by the examples of the past they may be able to save it from disaster. Although the examples of the past cast a certain light upon the nation's future pathway, nevertheless, should the leaders be mere opportunists, blinded by the attractions of immediate advantage, should they be unable to plan for the future, then there is grave danger of a vain repetition of the follies of former times. In that case there is no predicting where the misfortunes of the nation will end. Are there not innumerable instances in the pages of history where the decline of states has been due to such causes? What a pitiful reflection this is! Our Empire, however, possesses a strangely unique history. Although the origin of the nation is lost in the antiquity of thousands of years neither the hostile storms of adversaries nor the angry waves of their assault have ever been able to harm us. Innocent of revolution or revolt the Empire has steadily advanced along the path of its development, nor has it ever turned aside. Truly, this thought must produce boundless joy in the heart of every true subject of the Empire. Behold our Emperor firmly established upon his lofty throne whence he rules his subjects with paternal care. His loyal and filial subjects observe his commands and are only anxious lest they fail to act in accordance with his slightest wish. The land of Japan bears upon its breast an Emperor characterised by august virtues and a people who are his loyal subjects. There is none but delights to contemplate the eternal and glorious destiny of this Empire. As is frequently said, the country that preserves its individuality prospers, that country which loses it is quickly overthrown. Our sacred Empire stands aloft above all the world in unique and unparalleled sublimity. There must be some profound reason for its steady and unhindered advance through innumerable epochs to its present position of prosperity and power.

It is recorded that

Lord Sen of the country of Sei once asked Mencius whether it was true that Lord Tō had banished his Emperor Ketsu, and whether Lord Bu had overthrown his Emperor Chū. To which Mencius replied, "It is so written in the records". Lord Sen then questioned him further, saying, "Is it right for a subject to slay his lord?" Mencius then declared, "A man who repudiates benevolence is an outlaw, one who repudiates righteousness is a savage. Such are merely vulgar fellows. Although we hear of the execution of the vulgar Chū we have never yet heard of a subject slaying his lord".

But how can such things be? Loss of kingly rank does not

depend merely upon the character of the ruler. If the contention
of Mencius is correct then to banish a king who has forfeited
his authority through inefficiency or a vain display of power is
similar to banishing an ordinary subject. To a king who is not
a true king the subject owes no real allegiance. Furthermore,
to banish a ruler who is no true king and to take his place would
not be contrary to morality. It is true that such principles seem
to be popular in foreign lands where changes of dynasty occur,
and usurpations of power often take place accompanied by
bloodshed. It is not alone through the teachings of Mencius
that subjects in foreign countries have come to look upon such a
situation as natural and right. Such principles are found throughout the world. Indeed, it is only in our Empire that this
principle is not effective. Here ruler has always been ruler and
subject subject. No subject has ever aspired to be a ruler. Why
is it that no subject of this Empire has ever manifested this type
of ambition or this type of aspiration? This phenomenon is no
mysterious or inexplicable thing. We must recognise here one
of the special virtues and peculiar beauties which adorn our
sacred Empire. Our people have ever regarded the Emperor
as Emperor and from generation to generation they have served
him desiring nothing better than to die for his sake. They have
never ventured even in dreams to regard their Emperor as a
common or vulgar mortal. This ancient lord and vassal relation
so full of virtue has never fallen into desuetude and still remains
the unique glory of the Japanese nation.

Are not the ties of natural affection, which bind men to their
families and which keep ever green in their memories the
mountains and rivers of their native land, qualities which enhance
and adorn human nature? It is not that our families are so great
or our native landscapes so beautiful. It is our regard for them
that is of value. This quality of human nature is well reflected
in the ancient saying, "One's home is one's palace". While life
lasts men can never forget their families nor the landscape of
their childhood. In ancient times punishment for crime was
inflicted not only upon a man but upon his father, his wife,

and his children, or he was separated from them and banished
to some distant island. Such punishments display a deep
acquaintance with the intricacies of the human heart.

It is human nature to love one's home and relatives but these
are not the only motives which govern the lives of men. Men
cling instinctively to their clans, revere their ancestors, and
desire to share with others their joys and sorrows, their gain
and loss. So, too, men of the same race, whether yellow or
white, favour one another. For the same cause one tribe may
vaunt its superiority over another. Although these motives are
derived from the instincts of human nature they are nevertheless
frequently chaotic and mistaken. Although we regard a man's
willingness to fight for his own country as a worthy characteristic,
nevertheless, to do so without considering the constitution and
authorities of the state is unreasonable and not to be commended.
This becomes the more clear when we recall the fact that the
establishment of all these foreign countries and the founding
of their successive dynasties was brought about by war and
bloodshed. As for us, subjects of this Imperial state, the simple
honesty of our hearts accords well with the natural beauties of
our landscape. It is obvious that this Empire of Japan adorned
by these kindred beauties offers a striking contrast to all other
countries.

The subjects of our Emperor, whether officials or private
citizens, are united in heart in their anxiety to observe the
Imperial will. They devote themselves to the realisation of the
national policies of progress. Diligently applying themselves to
science and to the development and extension of business and
commerce they seek to do their part in furthering the harmonious
advance of civilisation throughout the world. Again, they unite
as one in cultivating the arts of war and in preparation for
conflict, so that in time of national emergency they may fulfil
their duty to their country. Although the history of other nations
displays successive periods of vigour and decline, prosperity and
national adversity, our Imperial state has never been subject to
such vicissitudes. When the Imperial command goes forth a

myriad blades flash out like dazzling snow, arrowheads beat down like summer rain, bullets fill the air like hail. Who can compare with the subjects of our Emperor as they spring forth to fulfil his martial commands with fearless mien? When such circumstances arise we are ready to meet the foe on every hand, we gladly carry our supplies a thousand miles and do not shrink from warfare upon the borders of distant lands. Rather we leap forward ready to endure all hardship in order that we may fulfil the demands of loyalty to our Emperor. Observing the strength of Japan rival nations have learned to fear her power. They are forced to admit the ever-expanding prestige of the Emperor. Russia and China, countries possessed of great territories, national wealth, and great armies, dared to infringe the honour of our nation, regardless of the claims of humanity and righteousness. In anger our Emperor mobilised his punitive arms and every subject subscribed to a blood pact to die at his command. In such manner has the magnificent courage of our people been ever displayed. Their bravery and valour is due first of all to loyal devotion to the will of the Emperor, to firm adherence to the claims of righteousness, and to instant readiness to sacrifice themselves for the sake of duty. Hence nothing has ever been lacking nor any blemish found in that unique lord and vassal relation which has persisted from the most ancient times. This fact must be obvious to all.

CHAPTER III

The Aspirations of the Subject

EVEN in the coldest weather the pine tree preserves its foliage. It is ever clothed in vivid green and lifts its lofty head like a verdant cloud throughout all the year. Shrouded in white mists, assaulted by piercing winds, scorched by the burning heat of summer it remains unchanged and continues to express its true nature with calm courage and patient endurance. The weak are strengthened by this sight and the vulgar ennobled. How fitting it is that we should adopt the pine tree as our pattern! How can we fail to honour the pine! Or let us turn our steps to the bamboo grove. Indeed, our sources of instruction are not few. How the bamboo plants emulate one another in their single-hearted struggle to attain heaven! Witnessing the purity of their growth we are inspired to achieve simplicity of heart and nobility of deed. When we look upon the hollow sections and the sturdy ridges of the stem we learn the lesson of the frank and unprejudiced mind and the necessity for firmly observing right principles. With what pains we must aspire to emulate the forthright character or the straightness of the springing bamboo!

When the snow falls and all the fields are covered with a blanket of white and every living thing suffers from the cold, there stands in the midst of desolation giving forth its delightful perfume that true model of all virtuous men. What is this but our plum blossom? The plum defies the hardest ice and cares for neither snow nor blighting frost. How vigorously it puts forth its blossoms regardless of all obstacles, spreading abroad the delightful odour of a glorious heritage! How can we with the toil of a whole lifetime emulate the beauty of such a model! Is it not right that we should learn of the plum blossom?

Under the warm sun of spring the whole land lies in tranquil peace and a hundred blossoms adorn the earth on every hand. Yet there is one among them which stands forth in splendid pre-eminence, stimulating the human heart and guiding it onward. This is none other than the marvel of the cherry blossom. It blooms the lord of a hundred flowers. Falling, it recalls to us the unique glories of knighthood. These are the characteristics of our cherry blossom. Those beautiful lines, "What is the spirit of Yamato[1] but the mountain cherry fragrant under the morning sun," spring involuntarily to our lips when we think of this resemblance. The subjects of our Emperor have received the spirit of progress from their ancestors and are prepared to assimilate the culture of the whole world. To die for a righteous cause is to submit to a burden no heavier than the down from the breast of a bird. Do not the deeds of the forty-seven knights of Akahō[2] illustrate this truth with

---

[1] The word Yamato as here used refers to the national ideals and their concrete manifestation throughout a long history of some 2500 years. This is the more usual modern connotation of the term. It is also used to designate the land and people of Japan. Originally it seems to have referred to the third great centre of colonisation secured by the dominant racial strain—the land conquered by the Emperor Jimmu in B.C. 660. Roughly speaking this is contained in the region between Lake Biwa and the Pacific. Exact data as to the limits of prehistoric Yamato and the period of its settlement have hitherto eluded the historian. Part of this area is still referred to frequently as Yamato. The term Yamato and the compound Yamatodamashii (spirit of Yamato) as employed by contemporary Japanese are often so richly symbolic that an adequate concise rendering into English is scarcely possible.

[2] The forty-seven knights of Akahō or Akō are more familiarly known as the forty-seven rōnin (masterless knights). Akō is the name of the ancestral domain of Lord Asano situated in what is now known as Hyōgo Prefecture. On the night of December 14th, 1702, the forty-seven knights under the leadership of Ōishi Kuranosuke attacked and killed in his yashiki Kira Yoshinaka whose arrogant and overbearing attitude had cast serious reflection upon the honour of Lord Asano leading eventually to his downfall and death. On April 21st, 1701, Asano Nagamori, Daimyō of Akō, had taken matters into his own hand and had attacked and wounded Kira Yoshinaka within the precincts of the Shōgun's palace. For this offence he was ordered to commit harakiri on the afternoon of the same day. As an act of mercy he was not informed of his failure to destroy his enemy. The loyal and selfless devotion of the retainers of Akō to a vendetta in which they had nothing to gain and everything to lose produced a profound impression at the time and has never ceased to be regarded as one of the finest products of the samurai code. Sympathy for the forty-seven knights was widespread and vigorous attempts were made in high places to save them from the death penalty. Unfortunately circumstances had prevented the forty-seven knights from complying with the regulation in the Legacy of Ieyasu in which it is expressly laid down that the slayer must notify the authorities (Hyōjōsho) of his intention. The whole story is justly regarded by the Japanese people as the most noteworthy

singular beauty? How brightly shines the spirit of Yamato in
our Empire! All the world must realise that the lofty pre-
eminence of this true spirit of the Japanese people is no sudden
or spontaneous growth.

The Empire of Japan, though it occupies a position no greater
than a fleck of foam upon the margin of the world, contains
within its bounds a paradise of purple mountains and crystal
waters, wherein the pine lifts its lofty top and the bamboo
flourishes, where the plum blossom fills the air with delightful
perfume and the cherry blooms in princely splendour. What a
fitting home for sages and heroes! As the saying has it, "Environment produces character". Men vary with their surroundings and their hearts reflect the phenomena of nature.
Again, the spirit of man alters his surroundings. He has power
to reform the circumstances of his environment. He who has
received his life out of this eastern nation of virtuous men, in
the midst of such an environment, cannot fail to live a life of
effort. He has received as ruler an Emperor unique among the
rulers of the earth. It is but natural that all who are privileged
to live in the midst of these beautiful influences should come
to manifest in their persons the true glory of our national spirit.

We are taught that there are four kinds of benevolence, the
benevolent grace of heaven, the benevolent grace of the nation
towards its subjects, the benevolent grace of parents towards
their offspring, and the benevolent spirit of society. To understand this benevolence is the basis of morality. Without this
knowledge men must remain brute beasts. We ever devote
ourselves to our Emperor and yield our lives to his will yet we
must ceaselessly mourn our insufficiency. Within our land
there is no region that does not belong to him, no human being
but acknowledges his sway. This is a true description of the

example of samurai loyalty to a feudal lord in the Tokugawa age. In 1744
the episode was dramatised by Takeda Izumo in the Chūshingura, probably
the greatest tragedy even written or enacted. The last noteworthy vendetta
occurred in 1868 and involved a samurai of high rank in the Mito clan. In
1873, however, katakiuchi or the practice of the vendetta was formally
abolished.

Empire of Japan, a fact which no subject ever forgets. Hence it is our duty to apply ourselves to the acquisition of culture and to practise the arts of war. Whether in the material sphere or in a spiritual sense we ever serve our country with singleness of heart. In time of danger we are ready to die at the Emperor's command. There is no greater honour for the subject than to offer his life for his country's cause. Thus by offering their lives in its service subjects repay the benevolent grace vouchsafed to them by their country. In the language of the Imperial poem, "How gallantly the Yamato spirit of our native land is manifest in time of need!" a sentiment which every subject reads with delight. During the epoch of Engen Kusunoki Masashige[1] received the Imperial command, succoured Nitta Yoshisada, and proceeded to attack the two Ashikaga rebels in the neighbourhood of Hyōgo.[2] He foresaw that the expedition would fail. After leaving the capital behind he preceded his force as far as the Sakurai post station and calling his son Masatsura to him laid upon him as his final command the task of destroying the rebels. Weeping, Masatsura desired to accompany him, but Masashige forbade it saying, "I leave you behind, not for my own sake but for the good of the country. You, however, do not comprehend, but cry like a young girl at parting. You are no son of mine". Masatsura, controlling his grief, obeyed his father. At that time he was only thirteen. Such incomparable loyalty is the highest type of public service. How can we adequately praise it! This spirit, however, is not the unique possession of the Kusunoki family. It is a virtue in which the myriad hearts of the subjects of Nippon have an equal share. How clearly is this displayed in the vigorous loyalty even of grooms and batmen during the recent war! The glory of the

[1] Known also as Nankō, the chivalrous defender of the Southern Court. See also note on page xxiv.
[2] The undoubtedly correct strategy of Kusunoki Masashige was neglected. As a result the Imperial forces were surrounded at a spot now included in the modern city of Kōbe. The Ashikaga rebels who had evidently taken the lessons of Dan-no-ura to heart owed their victory to the command of the sea and the unfortunate position of the Imperial army. The engagement took place on July 4th, 1336.

Japanese subject shines like clear, calm moonlight in a world of darkness.

Should one examine the innermost recesses of our being he would find neither personal ambition nor evil thought. Subjects have no thought but to obey the will of the Emperor and serve the interests of the state with all their might, seeking only to fulfil their high obligations. Truly our people manifest the beauty of whole-hearted service to the Empire. As the Emperor has written, "The loyalty to which our people aspire accords well with the mystic will of the gods". Do these words not acknowledge the sincere devotion of the Japanese people?

The spirit of our people when aroused is like the flashing lightning or the irresistible mountain avalanche. It is like a mighty river bursting its banks, like an awesome serpent, or swift as the leaping hare. Where else save among the subjects of this Empire can there be seen such a firm and unyielding attitude in the midst of this confused, complex, and ever-changing world; where else such steadfastness withstanding harmful influences, immovable and unconfused, firm as the mountains, calm as the quiet waters, and unalterably fixed upon the single duty of serving to the utmost the land of their fathers? According to the historical account, in the third year of Keiun[1] Wake no Kiyomaro[2] was banished to the western seas for his honesty. This incident arose from the fact that the archbishop Asomaro, having yielded to the blandishments of the priest Dōkyō, reported that the gods had declared that if the Imperial rank were conferred upon him (Dōkyō) the country would enjoy peace and prosperity. Kiyomaro was sent by the Empress to ascertain the will of the gods at the temple of Usa Hachiman in

---

[1] A.D. 769.

[2] It was after the second accession of the Empress Kōken to the throne that this incident occurred. The clever monk Dōkyō was her spiritual adviser and favourite. Dōkyō's confederate maintained that the oracle of Usa was the authority for his statement. The Empress selected the upright Kiyomaro from among her courtiers and sent him to verify the claim. It is related that Kiyomaro very nearly fell a victim to the vengeance of Dōkyō. Although he suffered mutilation he was rescued and sheltered by Fujiwara Momokawa. On the death of the Empress Dōkyō was himself banished to Shimotsuke.

the province of Buzen. Dōkyō called Kiyomaro aside and repeated the words of Asomaro, saying, "Should I become Emperor I would make you one of the highest officers of the land. If I do not become Emperor there is nought in store for you but a sword". On the way Kiyomaro met an honest man by the name of Toyonaga who exhorted him to tell the truth. Kiyomaro, deeply affected by his words, proceeded on his journey to Usa. After spending sleepless nights in prayer he returned and gave his reply to the court, saying, "I received in truth the very commands of the gods, in these words: 'Since the foundation of this nation there has been but one Imperial Line. How can this man Dōkyō, this wretched conspirator, dare to covet that Throne!'" At these words the Empress was speechless with astonishment and the throng of civil and military officials who were in attendance grew pale and burst into sweat at the audacity of Kiyomaro. How Kiyomaro is to be envied for his integrity! This tale of Kiyomaro's loyal heart which did not fail in its duty to the Throne is one of the beautiful treasures of all time. How truly this act exemplifies the real aspirations of the Japanese subject!

If a man makes no due preparation for the future he will not avoid disaster. It is thus with the nation. If we do not take advantage of the daily opportunities for progress, we manifest a foolishness as great as that which would put glue upon the "koto" bridges.[1] The future of such individuals and such nations is easily foreseen. To take advantage of the daily and monthly opportunities for progress, to be neither impeded by the mire of old customs, nor yet dazzled by new ideas, but rather to comprehend the new by a closer study of the old, and to prepare to receive the new while remembering the value of what is ancient, this is one of the peculiar glories of the Japanese character. This is the reason for the steady progress of the Empire toward its glorious destiny.

[1] An ancient Chinese saying. The koto is the Japanese harp. Each string is stretched on a movable bridge. There is obviously nothing more foolish, if the purpose is to produce music, than to glue the strings to the top of the bridge.

The Emperor has written, "We ever revere the ancient precedents while determining new policies". With what gratitude we should receive this sentiment! In the morning the people apply themselves to great affairs and in the evening they engage in contemplation. They do not neglect the preparation for the daily task whether in matters of learning or in the arts of war. While new culture fills the land and the country is not behind other nations in civilisation the people still remember to respect their ancestors and revere the Imperial Line. Stimulated by the noble example of the Imperial Ancestors, they obey their commands, anxious above all else lest they should disobey them. Truly, this is the way in which the people observe the teachings of Nippon Shindo, never straying aside from that True Way. The attitude of reverence which we Japanese subjects cherish towards our own ancestors and the Ancestors of the Imperial Line is clearly indicated in the well-known lines, "Though we know not the will of the gods yet our eyes brim with tears of thankfulness".

Words fail me to describe adequately the heart-aspirations of the Japanese subject. Despite its magnitude, however, I feel that it is worth while for me to attempt to write on this subject. How truly we subjects of Japan observe the precepts of our ancestors, contentedly applying ourselves to our several appointed tasks, and thus appropriately serving our Emperor! How well this is indicated in the words of the Emperor, "The people of this land observe the precepts of the ancient Emperors with single-hearted devotion!" and again, "Application to one's appointed task is the true duty of everyone whether high or low". Although the subjects strive to cultivate and ennoble their characters this never leads to arrogance. They seek to establish friendly relations with all foreign peoples and set up no barriers between themselves and others. As the Emperor has written, "When the four seas are brothers why should angry waves arise between them?" "Should the tender shoots of foreign plants or trees be tended carefully they will grow in luxurious competition in our garden." How true is this sentiment! Nevertheless, should the occasion for warfare arise, then, from the poor fisherman by the seaside to the lonely mountaineer, all will come forward eager to seek an opportunity to display their courage in the service of their country. The subjects of Japan whether from the waterside or from the mountain are ever ready to serve their Emperor with their last breath. Weapon in hand they will devote themselves unreservedly to driving out the enemies of their Sovereign. I do not hesitate to maintain that this is the true spirit of the subjects of Japan. The people of Japan can never be satisfied even with the loyalty of Hakui and Shukusei who, refusing to listen to treachery against their lord, withdrew into the mountains of Shuyō and subsisted upon fern shoots because they would eat nothing produced by the land which lay under the heel of the usurping dynasty.[1] So long as there is blood in their veins and flesh upon their bones even the sacrifice of life itself must fail to content the subjects of Japan while the enemies of the Emperor are unsubdued. I firmly believe that I make no mistake in declaring these to be the true aspirations of the subjects of Japan.

[1] The brothers Hakui and Shukusei were subjects of the Emperor Chū of the In dynasty (China). A powerful vassal by the name of Bu overthrew his sovereign Chū, thus founding the Shū dynasty. The sentiment of loyalty was strong in the two brothers who refused to recognise the usurper. They vowed never to eat food produced by the subjects of the tyrant and retired into the mountains where they subsisted on fern shoots until they died—a slight euphemism for a speedy demise induced by starvation.

CHAPTER IV

The Duties of the Subject

THERE is enthroned on high one who fulfils the lofty prerogatives of Emperor, with august wisdom, sacred dignity, and valorous courage. Below there live his myriad subjects possessed of innate talents and well aware of their duties, who perpetually devote their whole energy to the accomplishment of their daily tasks. How glorious that rule and how beautiful those traditions! In other countries their equal is not to be found. No foreign people may successfully imitate these unique qualities. Peerless from of old and unique in the whole world is the Empire of Japan. Heaven has not placed man on earth to live in lonely isolation but in order that he may live collectively and work out his destiny in social groups. This is the origin of human society and the basis of national organisations. The strength and weakness of a group depends upon the strength or weakness of the elements of which it is composed. Again, the strength of the group depends upon the power of union and cohesion existing in the elements. Should the elements themselves be weak and deficient in the power of union then overthrow and downfall are a foregone conclusion. Although men say that the power of a nation depends upon the inaccessibility of its mountains and the suitability of its shores for embarkation, nevertheless true strength is only gained when there are added to these natural advantages the initial strength of the human elements and their power of uniting with other elements. The successful development of society, the prosperity of the group, the auspicious destiny of the nation all arise from these two considerations.

That the rise and fall of nations, their peaceful prosperity or their adversity in time of war arise from the strength or weakness, the relative superiority or inferiority of the elements which compose them, becomes abundantly clear as we examine the pages of human history. The short-lived prosperity of Greece, and the fact that the power which spread the Roman civilisation over the world soon declined leaving nothing but monuments of its grandeur behind, are excellent examples of this contention. The wealth and power for which England and America are famed has not been a mere spontaneous growth. Nevertheless, they too illustrate this view. It is an error to argue from their present condition that their prosperity will endure for ever. Their history has been full of tragic misery, usurpations, and dynastic strife. These incidents crowd one upon the other. Dynasty succeeds dynasty and clan wrests power from its rival clans. There is in these nations a constant variation of power and they are utterly unable to avoid that working of the natural law by which the new ever supplants the old. Among these people there is but slight interest taken in observing the formalities of ancestral worship or in maintaining the integrity of the state. They are content merely to serve the reigning family of the hour and to cling to the powerful faction. Such a state of affairs is clearly exemplified in the case of China and Korea. There is, indeed, no greater danger to be encountered by the state than this inherent weakness of its component elements, and their inability to cohere. If the elements are weak in this sense the nation will surely be overthrown. Those who are responsible for maintaining the national organisation must study the matter closely, for failure here will render any plan for perpetuating it as foolishly ineffective as though a man were to paint a cat and imagine that he had produced a tiger. It would be like dreaming of a dragon and finding a snake. In the history of foreign powers errors of this nature are clearly evident. What words, therefore, are adequate to describe our unique Empire, unchanged and unchangeable, blest on the one hand with a single immutable Imperial Line and on the other with courageously devoted subjects, who ceaselessly fulfil their duties and overthrow the enemies of the Empire! This phenomenon is due to the aid of heaven mediated to us through our Emperor, coupled with that loyal service rendered by the people of Yamato, which shall continue unaltered as long as heaven and earth shall endure.

From the woodcutter upon the mountains to the fisherman who turns the seaweed and collects salt by the shore what man is there that neglects his vocation? Some devote their lives to driving the locomotive, others to piloting the steamboat. Still others devote their lives to the pursuit of learning, lecturing in the university or wielding the pointer in the public school. In their tireless preoccupation wealth and renown are ignored. In the world of commerce and trade the people apply themselves to their tasks from starlit morn till moonlit eve, in order that the true interest and profit of the nation may be served. They are not blinded by the empty vanities of this world. In public life they serve the state in both the civil and the military sphere, in private life by pen and spoken word. When they shape the policies of the nation they are actuated by a whole-hearted desire to serve the Imperial state. They are not led astray by selfish motives. The same spirit is found in the ranks of the priesthood. It is displayed by all who bear the friar's staff, as well by those who through the medium of devotional writings seek to provide the people with the consolations of religion. Every subject of the Empire is content with his lot, taking care not to neglect his calling. From of old down to the present day this has been the unchanging spirit of the subjects of our Empire. When we consider the question carefully we realise that this felicity is due to reverent obedience to the commands of the Emperor, to the right use of the weapons of warfare, and to the progressive assimilation of new elements of civilisation.

When we centre our reverent contemplation upon our nation, the land of Toyo-ashihara-no-mizuho,[1] we realise that it is but a small island in the midst of the ocean, threatened by angry waves. With a history already three thousand years old our nation still stands forth before the world like a perfect golden vessel bearing no blemish inflicted by hostile hands. Those who would write the history of mankind or limn the atlas of the

---

[1] A term derived from the early legendary period of Japanese history. Its use here in reference to modern Japan carries with it sacred implications from the early "Age of the Gods".

globe cannot neglect it. That such learned savants have come to regard this land as an area of importance reflects honour upon our Empire. The causes which have produced this noble Empire are first of all the possession of a uniquely sacred Emperor who nourishes us his people in a manner unparalleled in any other country. On the other hand we, the subjects, hold our Emperor in reverent awe, regarding him as the central object of our national life. Through him all his subjects are united more closely than by lacquer or glue. United we are strong with the combined strength of a bundle of ten arrows which cannot be broken. Unity such as this is not to be found in the history of any other people. A ruler thus characterised leads a people who fear neither floods nor flames nor flying bullets. Depending solely upon the right they walk the path of truth without swerving, acknowledging but one duty, that of obedience to the Imperial commands. Thus were they able to repulse the Mongolian invasion of old. Thus, more recently, they were able to overcome the Empire of China. How was it possible for such a small nation to compass such deeds? It is due to the firmly established relation between Emperor and subject. It is due to the peculiar virtue of the subjects by which they are able to keep the true path with loyal hearts. It is because they never neglect the virtue of public service. It is hardly necessary to emphasise this point further. All of these advantages are due to the special grace accorded to our Emperor by heaven. Thus shall the people of Yamato serve their divine Emperor and enjoy true prosperity as long as heaven and earth endure. When, on the fourth day of January in the fifteenth year of Meiji (1882), the present Emperor vouchsafed to his soldiers his Imperial Edict he declared:

I am your Commander-in-Chief, you are my strong arms. You shall regard me as your head, then shall our relation be close and deep. By the grace of Heaven I protect and rule this land. Whether I shall adequately fulfil my duty to the Ancestors depends upon your fidelity. Should the prestige of the country suffer diminution you shall sorrow with me. Should our power increase and our glory shine more brightly then I with you shall share that glory. If you unite with me in fidelity to duty, if you devote your strength to the protection of the nation, then our people shall enjoy prolonged peace and prosperity. Our courage and power shall illuminate the whole earth.

His soldiers obeyed the Imperial commands in accordance with the instruction contained in this Imperial Edict. The demands of loyalty and righteousness are heavier upon their conscience than the weight of great mountains. To die in the Emperor's service is a duty as easy to bear and as light as a feather. Observing the rules of etiquette the soldier respects his superiors and is benevolent towards his inferiors, while mutual esteem pervades the hearts of all. They accord high respect to militant courage, and ever conceive their duties with clarity. They cultivate physical courage and plan their manœuvres with anxious care, neither neglecting the weak enemy nor yet fearing the strong. Each and every one hopes above all else to quit himself like a courageous and knightly warrior. Holding mutual trust in high regard they keep their promises. Remembering their duties they regard frugality as of the utmost importance and avoid all luxurious habits. On the other hand, avoiding miserly penuriousness they aspire to achieve true nobility of character. The world respects them for their militant courage. Pursuing this path they devote themselves whole-heartedly to fulfilling the duty which they owe to their country. To serve the Emperor with such earnest devotion is the highest ambition of our soldiery. Because this spirit is displayed throughout the Empire all the people gladly unite in the fullest and truest service of the Imperial state. This happy service rendered by the subject is due to the sacred character of our Emperor, who jealously guards his people with that heavenly grace that has been vouchsafed to him.

The subjects of the Emperor, by observing well the Constitution, the Regulations Governing the Imperial Household, and the instructions contained in the Imperial commands, are able to fulfil their duty with single-hearted devotion. Thus they successfully prosecute their professions whether in the spheres of learning or of war, of agriculture, industry or commerce. By their true devotion they hope to repay and requite the Imperial benevolence. This is the true and unique Way which the subjects of the Empire of Japan must observe and follow. From this Way no single subject of the Empire can ever wander astray no matter what the circumstances of his life.

CHAPTER V

Concerning Loyalty and Filial Piety in General

WE are taught that loyalty and filial piety are the foundations of human virtue and the sources of the five sacred relations. If we set aside loyalty and filial piety there is no other source available for morality. In the first instance righteousness and benevolence depend upon them and in the second the individual relations are derived from them. It is the active principle of loyalty and filial piety which vitalises the people of Japan. For this reason teachers of morals past and present devote themselves to a detailed study of loyalty and filial piety, making the observance of these virtues the basis of their systems. In my opinion, however, such expositions are utterly at fault. I have been forced to conclude that their erroneous assumptions must lead them at length into many fundamental misconceptions. As I have already twice maintained, loyalty, in the widest sense of the term, is the only source of moral action. As my ideas on loyalty in general must already be abundantly clear I shall here take a further step and endeavour to explain what I believe to be the inner meaning of these two doctrines. I shall also endeavour to provide examples which will prove that my former contention is correct.[1]

If we analyse loyalty we find two kinds. One is the source of all ethical action, and the other of the sacrificial service rendered to the Emperor. Let it be understood that in this chapter I shall employ the word loyalty in the latter sense. Under the widespreading heavens and in every corner of our land, from the woodcutter who sleeps among the mountains to the fisherman who is the companion of the restless waves, the people of Japan without exception regard the Imperial Line with reverential awe, and are ever ready to devote their lives to the supreme claims of patriotism. This is not merely a tradition

[1] For General Nogi's marginal comments on this passage see Appendix, paragraph 3.

handed down by our ancestors. Even among the highly developed and cultured citizens of modern Japan it is a vital principle. This spirit is the life motive of the Japanese people, their very flesh and blood. Since the foundation of the world and the establishment of this country there have arisen none who would dare to controvert this statement. Truly, the essential spirit of loyalty in the Japanese subject is so well understood and recognised that it would be a foolish waste of time for me to labour this point further.

Teachers of ethics and morals for the most part regard loyalty and filial piety as parallel virtues. They make them equally the two fundamental principles of ethics. They make these words the texts of their lectures on morals. This has always been the case up to the present. They cannot cast off this habitual error even to-day. This strikes me as very strange. In my opinion it is a great error to place filial piety on a level with loyalty. Filial piety should be placed in the same class as fraternal affection, domestic harmony, fidelity to one's friends, and the love of humanity, and should be enforced as equally obligatory with these. This I regard as the suitable order. There may formerly have been a reason for giving special importance to filial piety but it is certain that a great mistake has been made. Why should fraternal affection, domestic harmony, fidelity to one's friends, and humanitarian sentiments be so neglected? I should like to enquire whether the relation of filial piety itself does not depend upon the relation of domestic harmony? Again, is not domestic felicity the source of fidelity between friends, and the root of humanitarian feeling? Indeed, even from the point of view of time, if we realise that domestic felicity precedes filial piety, then to regard it as inferior is putting the cart before the horse. It would not be wrong to point out that the essential balance has been lost sight of in these teachings.

From ancient times those who enforced the virtue of filial piety maintained that it was the means of fulfilling the duty of repaying and requiting our parents for their kindness in bringing us up. According to these teachers, children are created by their parents and are brought up by them, hence the benevolence of parents is more lofty than the highest mountains, and deeper than the ocean depths. Because children have received such measureless and boundless benefits they should endeavour to repay them in direct ratio. Although these arguments appear very clever a little analysis shows that they may easily lead men astray. This is a point which every one should clearly grasp. If we must fulfil the duty of filial piety because we have received benefits from our parents the fundamental principles of ethics are endangered. Serious differences of opinion concerning filial piety must result and there is some danger that the virtue of filial piety may fall into disrepute. If it is claimed that a man must fulfil the claims of filial piety because of benefits received from his parents what shall we say of the unfilial child who maintains that he has already completely repaid the benevolence of his parents? Or what shall we say of the son who admits having been brought into the world by his parents but repudiates the claims of filial piety, on the ground that he was a foster child from his earliest years and has not benefited by that parental benevolence, which the world regards as higher than the most lofty mountains? If we are to accept the dictum of such teachers what are we to say in these cases? If we should continue to maintain that the virtue of filial piety is more lofty than the mountains and deeper than the ocean and teach that this doctrine demands a mathematically exact repayment of the benevolent kindness of parents then it is quite possible that such inhuman and unethical persons as we have described may appear. If this filial piety, which is one of the most important principles of ethics, should be seriously questioned the order of society will be upset and domestic peace disturbed. It is of the utmost importance to prevent the occurrence of such a misfortune. For this reason I am attempting to rescue the virtue of filial piety from its dangerous position. I am really trying to eliminate all grounds for opposition to filial piety. I desire to insist upon the necessity for securing a firm foundation for its enforcement. I desire that every one should believe that wherever the relation of parent and child exists it is important and useful to establish the claims of the ethical principle of filial piety upon the child. When once the true filial relation is established it can never be destroyed. If we make this indestructible relation the basis of an ethical principle then we can press the claims of filial piety upon children and arouse interest in this virtue. If we take such a course the unfilial son can hardly have any argument left. It is my earnest hope that the dogma that the child fulfils its duty to the parent simply because it is a child should be firmly established and remain for ever unchanged, in order that it may become the sound basis for future well-being not only in the individual home, but in the nation as well.

CHAPTER VI

Loyalty

F AR to the east of Europe there lies, on the edge of the
Pacific,[1] a lovely shining Island Empire, whose beauty
dazzles the eye of all beholders. In the Empire of Japan,
coeval with heaven and earth, the people enjoy endless peace
and vie with one another in their effort to increase her glory
and renown. Though infinitely small in area the knightly valour
of her sons astounds the whole world. Such is our great Empire
of Japan, a phenomenon unique under the wide heavens.

Each son of that Empire offers true-hearted loyalty to his
Emperor, never neglecting his duties nor slighting the Imperial
commands. The people serve their Emperor with greater
affection than the child accords to its mother, with greater fear
than the trembling son feels for his stern father. Our Emperor,
rich in divine virtue, wisdom, and valour, ever rules his subjects
with affectionate solicitude. He is like the sun, shining in the
heavens, and shedding its glorious light upon all living things.
There is nothing lacking in the benevolent winds or the kindly
rains of his overflowing grace. His subjects cannot fail to be
affected by such goodness. We gladly acknowledge that heaven
has graciously created these subjects for such an Emperor and
has granted to them an Emperor such as ours. It requires no
deep research to comprehend the source of this unbroken
Succession and the ever-increasing glory of the Imperial
Destiny.

When we enquire into the causes that lead to the alternate
rise and fall of nations, their periods of greatness and their
epochs of adversity, we find, although there are many factors
to be considered, that the most important one is the character
of the people. If the people are lacking in character they are
nothing but savages and barbarians. Their glory will be as

---

[1] For General Nogi's marginal comments on this passage see Appendix,
paragraph 4.

evanescent as that of the flower that blooms in the morning. The overthrow and dissipation of their power and prestige is inevitable. If the leaders of a nation do not exert themselves to the utmost to cultivate the character of the people the future of the nation can be easily foretold. Nations whose peoples lack true strength and character quickly lose their rank in the midst of rival powers. Lacking internal unity such peoples will be unable to escape the fate of absorption and subjugation by their rivals. Nations possessing great resources and splendid armies but lacking in character are bound to employ their power ruthlessly and selfishly. For a time they may rejoice in their prosperity but it is a prosperity which obscures the light of heaven. Such a nation can never long prevail. It is bound to fall by its own violence and stumble in its own strength. After such nations have overreached themselves true peace may be expected to return to earth once more. How important, therefore, it is to cultivate true character. That nation which desires continued prosperity must never neglect the cultivation of national character. If it ever loses it its decline and downfall are certain. The remains of such national disaster are strewn plentifully throughout the pages of human history. No matter how great the ascendancy, no matter how exceptional the valour, courage and power alone without character are not to be commended nor can they be long maintained. Honour and power will soon desert the country that puts its trust in such things. Ancestral ceremonies will be forsaken and national fortresses abandoned. The courts of such a people will fill with wild grasses and they will become the laughing-stock of mankind. Is not the fate of such countries which for a time vaunt their barbarous strength a pitiable one?

The present differs chiefly from the past in that we possess more of the material benefits of civilisation. The means of transportation have been perfected and the countries of the earth have all entered the same arena of the struggle for existence. How fierce is that struggle! How deplorable it is!

As civilisation advances the struggle for existence takes on many changing aspects. In practical affairs it is reflected in commerce, in industry, and in agriculture. In the more abstract field of human activities weapons of conflict are sharpened in the sphere of literature and culture. Nations live in a state of armed peace and carry on continually a kind of peaceful warfare. Every element of society is eternally on guard. These words describe the field of human activity as it is to-day. The strong regard the claims neither of righteousness nor of humanity. They regard nothing but their own selfish interests. They desire to attach to themselves the possessions of others and to destroy other peoples. They are unabashed in their brutality. They glory in their selfish strength and act as though no one else had a right to exist. Glorying in their brutal power their evil desires know no bounds. This state of affairs cannot but arouse our highest indignation. We who are subjects of a divinely appointed Emperor, who observes the claims of righteousness and humanity, who straightens what is crooked, who fulfils his obligations toward heaven and earth, before whom there is neither weak nor strong, neither poor nor rich, who has received his Imperial Mission from heaven, and who possesses the virtue of benevolence, we, the subjects of this Emperor and this Empire, cannot look upon these evils without protest, nor can we avoid the conviction that he also must inevitably condemn them.

A single day of selfish pleasure may result in a hundred years of misfortune and bitter suffering. How much more perilous is the present situation. Numerous foes exist on every side, who, like raging tigers, unrestrained by considerations of righteousness or benevolence, will never be satisfied till they have destroyed their prey. Under such circumstances international treaties cannot be depended upon, nor can reliance be placed on promises of peace. The habitation of the weak soon becomes the lair of the leopard. The natural defences of rivers and mountains are no longer sufficient to prevent the advent of enemies nor can the dangers of the deep restrain them. The savage Russians, filled with senseless pride, feed their horses upon the fields of Manchuria, water them in the Yalu, and proceed as though the country were uninhabited. On beholding their evil deeds and their ill-mannered invasion the Chinese and the Koreans are not alone in their indignation. Both the old and great nation and the small and weak one were heedlessly led astray by fair words and deceived by flattery. Grasping at a momentary pleasure they neglected to realise the inevitable sorrows which would follow. When they had fallen into dangerous circumstances they were greatly troubled as to how they should deal with the situation, and they tried to act as though it were not too late to extricate themselves. What a pitiful debâcle!

Although the area of our Empire is as small as the palm of the hand the national spirit fears neither time nor space. When China set out to possess herself of the eight provinces of Korea our Emperor commanded his loyal subjects and sent forth his righteous armies to the aid of that country, utterly defeating the aims of China. They were forced to capitulate and were left no means of breaking forth a second time.[1] The august virtues of our Emperor are ever thus revealed. Again, when the storm clouds of war gathered and the Russians imposed their selfish will upon the coasts of Asia, despising the power of this nation, we showed that we feared neither ancient eagle nor ravening wolf. Our righteous armies sprang across the intervening seas, scaled the mountains, forded the mighty rivers, and, after innumerable and repeated assaults, finally watered their horses on the very shores of Beikal, and unfurled the national emblem upon the Urals. An unwarranted contempt became the occasion for limning upon the pages of history the record of that glorious achievement whereby we brandished our weapons upon the very borders of the occident. Every subject of the Empire realised his unavoidable duty. Obeying the commands of the Emperor to the last detail, and endeavouring above all else to avoid casting reproach upon his decrees, we advanced in the east and attacked in the west. In this supreme effort the true heart of

---

[1] For General Nogi's marginal comments on this passage see Appendix, paragraph 5.

the subject was revealed. This is well expressed in the poem:
"Unless we seek diligently in the deepest mountain fastness the
true beauty of the autumn leaves is not revealed".

The subjects of the Emperor devote themselves diligently to
carrying out his commands, much less do they ever oppose
them. Each and all desire to be filled with the spirit of righteous
courage, to display honest endeavour throughout their lives, and
to be always ready to fall in the service of the country. Each
one desires to be a pattern of the loyal subject and the true
knight. The ideals of the Kusunoki family are the ideals of every
subject. The heart of Shigemori is the heart of every son of
Japan. These ideals are revealed in innumerable knightly deeds,
whose fragrance is like the myriad clusters of the cherry blossoms,
and in the hundred-tempered steel of our valorous blades.
Above there rules such an Emperor, below there exists such a
people. For the three thousand years that have elapsed since
its founding our Empire has made daily advance toward its
glorious destiny. Led ever forward by the good powers of
heaven and earth she has never lost territory to a foreign
conqueror, nor has any subject ever been made prisoner by an
alien power. With such a history and such a destiny it is but
natural that neither the talons nor the tusks of the birds and
beasts of prey that surround her have ever left their mark upon
her fair possessions.

Our country has ever been known as a land of noble men
possessing an Emperor rich in august virtue, and citizens who
render him true-hearted service and are characterised by the
most perfect loyalty. Should worm-like foreign reptiles dare to
insult the dignity of the Emperor or to pollute his virtuous name
the spirit of heaven and earth cannot refrain from meting out
punishment, nor can his subjects withhold their indignant ire.
They will never rest until they have avenged the national insult.
With such an Emperor, such a people, and such a nation there
is nothing to fear from the vicissitudes which afflict mundane
affairs, nor need we fear the angry waves of hostile foes. That
each should be contented with his lot and ever ready to offer his

life for his country is not only the heart's desire of every loyal subject of the Empire but also his greatest glory.

To further the interests of the country and extend its power there have never been lacking means. Destruction of the weak and oppression of the feeble, however, have never been the methods of the people of Yamato. They cannot overlook the acts of those evildoers who lawlessly injure neighbouring countries without regard for their national rights and prerogatives. The subjects of our Emperor are trained in a universal service to go forth as a virtuous army and to fight as a united nation in the cause of righteousness, and they are determined to sacrifice their lives, if need be, for the Emperor's sake. With hearts full of loyalty and bodies overflowing with righteous determination they leap to obey his commands. Is not every one who has received the gift of life in this land like the hero of the poem "Whether I float as a corpse upon the waters, or sink beneath the grasses of the mountain side I willingly die for the cause of the great Ruler"? Who is there that does not long to be a loyal knight? How happy are the subjects of Japan!

Such is the heart of our people. For a thousand years unchanged this spirit has been displayed in filial piety, connubial felicity, mutual trust, love of humanity, in frugality, and in loyal service. From frozen north to torrid south the subjects obey the Emperor, nor have they ever yet suffered defeat or felt fatigue in his cause. For three thousand years this Island Empire has stood, like a flawless vessel of gold, or an evergreen pine which rears its crest in inviolate and changeless verdure amidst the withered foliage of the surrounding forest. How glorious is that sight!

CHAPTER VII

Filial Piety

OUR birth into this world depends, of course, upon our parents. By the nurture and upbringing of our parents we are what we are to-day. It is reasonable that purest affection between parents and offspring should ever well abundantly and incessantly from the depths of our natures. Having received their lives from their parents, to be filial to them, to serve them, and to obey them are the fundamental duties of all who call themselves true men. It is but natural that both in the east and west, of old and in the present, wise men should agree that filial piety is the fundamental obligation of human morality.

From the fortunate gentleman in his noble mansion to the hard-working peasant in his humble hovel there is none that would seek to avoid this obligation. From the days of prehistoric barbarism and savagery down to the most advanced and recent civilisation, in every age in fact, men have been exhorted to obey the precepts of filial piety. No matter to what age or locality we carry our enquiry we find no tendency to neglect this principle. Filial piety arises with mankind and accompanies his eternal destiny. It is an immutable and everlasting principle which must always be enforced, for it is one of those beautiful virtues which adorn human society. If we would avoid disgracing our humanity we must cultivate this virtue, which arises from the natural affection existing between parents and children.

As human beings we are born into the relation of parent and child, and the filial obligations are inevitable. Public instruction may vary in different nations. In some the individual point of view is stressed, in others the humanitarian, the socialistic, or the national point of view is predominant. Nevertheless, in every country the obligations of children with respect to their parents are insisted upon. Nowhere is obedience to the claims of filial piety omitted. Where filial piety is neglected no close relation can exist between parents and children, and the individual is therefore unable to achieve a truly satisfactory type of life. Under such conditions humanity is bound to lose those pre-eminent qualities which make men the lords of creation. Under such conditions society is bound to disintegrate. A nation in which such conditions exist is headed for destruction. The happy consummation of the individual life, the beneficial increase of population, the prosperity of society, and a truly flourishing national life all depend upon this primary virtue of filial piety. We cannot afford to neglect it for a single day.

Filial piety is the way by which a child fulfils its obligations to its parents. Wherever the relation of parent and child exists, there also is the necessary obligation of filial obedience. All who are children must follow this way through life. Should they ever stray aside from it they must necessarily lose a fundamental characteristic of their humanity. The truth of that way is not to be sought afar, it is to be found near at hand. The peace of the whole nation depends upon the tranquillity of the individual household. The tranquillity of the household depends upon the integrity of its members. If the household enjoys tranquillity how can the nation fail to be characterised by peaceful prosperity? If integrity characterises the members of the household how can filial piety fail to be observed therein? If integrity characterises the individual members and filial piety is found in the group then the future destiny of the country is assured. We subjects of the Emperor have been born into a society which exists by divine sanction. Hence we must cultivate filial piety, manifest loyalty, and unfailingly serve the destiny of our country even if it should cost us our lives.

From of old those who have taught the precepts of morality have placed filial piety first in order. Filial piety is indeed the axle upon which revolves the wheel of human morality. Those who lack filial piety are not worthy to be called the lords of creation. Those who would polish and enhance the beauties of virtue which adorn humanity must first of all endeavour to perfect themselves in filial piety. Filial piety is like the root and

the stem of the plant. If the stem is not trained the branches
and the foliage will grow into wild confusion. Degenerate
persons who do not acknowledge the claims of filial piety have
ever been treated as the most miserable of outcasts. Thus, if
we who are subjects of this Empire desire to become truly loyal
citizens, we must observe the obligations of filial piety. If the
children of the state observe the duties of this virtue, and the
parent and child relation is firmly established, the pillars of
society will be strengthened. True filial piety in the child results
in true loyalty in the subject. Loyal subjects of this Empire are
always filial children, and filial children are never anything but
loyal subjects.

The observance of filial piety increases the prosperity of the
Empire. We only practise filial piety that we may produçe truly
loyal subjects. A system of filial obligations opposed to the
commands of the Emperor could never exist among us. True
filial piety and true loyalty are never opposed. Provided that
there are no mutually exclusive principles in these teachings no
torturing doubts can arise as to whether men may be both filial
and loyal at the same time. We must always be loyal subjects.
For this reason the subjects of the Empire can never afford to
cultivate a filial piety which is at variance with loyalty.[1] Circumstances may arise when we shall be obliged to refuse
unreasonable filial demands on the part of our parents. We
must never hesitate as subjects in the vigorous display of loyalty
and patriotism. Let us, therefore, be both loyal and filial.
Although to realise both virtues is our obvious duty we can
never permit any interpretation of filial piety which would
conflict with loyalty. After all, our primary end is to be loyal
subjects.

In form, filial piety is a matter of lineal descent. It is a duty
rendered to parents, grandparents, and great-grandparents. This
human virtue of service to parents on the part of descendants is
called filial piety. When regarded from within, however, filial

[1] For General Nogi's marginal comments on this passage see Appendix,
paragraph 6.

piety, although it has many aspects, is seen to mean loyalty.[1] We must realise that filial piety exists to perfect the character of the truly loyal subject. The cultivation of filial piety is not for the sake of the individual or the single member of society, nor does it depend upon any individual beliefs. It is cultivated for the purpose of realising true and complete loyalty. It is cultivated in order that there may be no defect in the loyal subject. With this end in view we who are subjects cultivate character and personality, seek to gain the confidence and trust of men, and strive to attain renown, thus showing honour to our parents. We endeavour to preserve our bodies from harm and take pains with our behaviour in order that we may not disappoint their expectations. To afford our parents spiritual and material satisfaction is the first and essential duty, as every one knows.

How must we who are born the children of these parents, we who are subjects living in this favoured epoch, strive to maintain the integrity of our characters! The true purpose implicit in the obligations of loyalty and filial piety is indeed the maintenance and realisation of those true characteristics which distinguish the subject of the Emperor. In conclusion I repeat, there are no two separate Ways of loyalty and filial piety open to us. For us who are subjects of this Empire there is only one Way, the Way of Loyalty.[2] We cultivate filial piety simply in order to round out and embellish that loyalty, not for the sake of filial piety itself. To cultivate a filial piety of which loyalty is the central motive must be our daily endeavour.[3] We should strive to attain this perfection even in our dreams. Although it has been said that the loyal subject comes from the house of the filial son, I am convinced that it is preferable to say that the filial son comes from the house of the loyal subject. We must never forget that we cultivate filial piety not as mere human beings but as loyal subjects.

[1] For General Nogi's marginal comments on this passage see Appendix, paragraph 7.
[2] See Appendix, paragraph 8.
[3] See Appendix, paragraph 9.

CHAPTER VIII

The Basis of the Imperial State

BEHOLD the lofty mansion soaring above the clouds! How was it established? Can we not easily imagine the toil and the effort of the artisans who constructed it? How strong must be those walls and that roof that it has stood so long! How important is the firmness of the supporting pillars! How perfect, above everything else, must have been the laying of the foundation stones! Even in the construction of a great building such careful preparations are necessary. A careful builder always warns us that we must not thoughtlessly take up edged tools. Even in the mouth of an ignorant amateur such a warning demands the closest attention.

Again, consider the preparation necessary before undertaking a lengthy journey or an expedition. How carefully must the individual who is about to set forth pore over the map, study the climate, accumulate his equipment, and busily occupy himself with all manner of preparations. The activity of his mind and body is amazing. How much more should he who sojourns in the house of life, desiring to prolong his days therein, occupy his mind with inconceivably anxious thought and earnest preparation!

There is now in the world a multitude of states. They all seek to perpetuate their national organisations for a myriad years. They desire an unbroken celebration of their festivals and anniversaries. Although such is the universal hope of those who establish nations it is nevertheless an exceedingly difficult thing to realise. In the Sengoku era the country of Shin dominated the whole earth, yet through lack of great vassals this supremacy was soon lost. Such examples are frequently met with in the history of the world. How can they avoid disaster who have no carefully considered plan for the future? How can they avoid failure who heedlessly undertake the business of ruling and merely dream of perpetuating imperial power? Even the establishment of the most ephemeral state requires the most strenuous effort on the part of its founders. To have founded solidly an Imperial rule which has endured for a myriad years, and to have maintained throughout the success of such a vast undertaking may well seem unbelievable, yet no one acquainted with the facts can deny that there is such a country.

Among the motives of those who desire to establish states are these, the desire to satisfy ephemeral ambition, the longing to display cleverness and ability, and the fondness for the exercise of irresponsible power and authority. Such individuals regard only their own selfish interests. They do not plan ahead even for a century. Nevertheless, they boldly aspire to the office of an emperor. Due to such limitations of vision they die for the most part without having accomplished any great designs. History contains examples of this kind without number. Their failure is, of course, not to be wondered at. Great imperial designs depend for their success upon careful planning for the future and upon a superhuman character and wisdom in the founder. In this respect even that Golden Age of Gyō and Shun is defective.[1] Even the powerful emperors Bun and Bu and their great retainer Shūkō leave something to be desired, nor is there any need that we should extravagantly praise them.

To found an Empire which shall stand for a myriad years requires not only the highest authority and virtue; such an undertaking calls for the most superior talents and the most penetrating wisdom and foresight in the founder. Such a founder must possess those qualities which will win the un-grudging and voluntary reverence and respect of succeeding generations of subjects. It is only by the most superhuman talents and wisdom that this Empire has been established in a world of sharp competition where the drawn sword stands before and the keen axe behind. You will not find the equal of this

---

[1] The Chinese Emperors Gyō, Shun, and U ruled over the destinies of China in the so-called Golden Age (*circa* B.C. 2400). Under the wise and beneficent rule of these monarchs the country enjoyed prolonged peace and great prosperity. Among the Chinese they are the prototypes of the perfect ruler.

nation in Europe or America, nor yet in Asia. It is this Japanese Empire of ours, situated here upon the extreme borders of the Asiatic continent, which alone fulfils all these conditions.

According to our historical records:

Before the creation and differentiation of heaven and earth, when all was yet like the mingled elements of an egg, the molten mass contained a germ by whose activity the light elements arose and became heaven, while the murky elements congealed and became earth. Thereupon was born the divine being Kami-toko-tachi-no-mikoto or Ame-no-minakanushi-no-mikoto, who was the first divinity of creation.[1]

Thus our Empire had its source in these primeval and most ancient times. Thus in the prehistoric age our Empire was already founded. In that distant antiquity the Imperial design was completely established. We who are subjects of this land are not alone in recalling this fact with reverent awe. The peoples of other nations regard it with envy.

The Imperial Ancestors have founded our country on a basis broad and everlasting. It is to be feared that our shallow perceptions fail to comprehend this great phenomenon. Such an august enterprise must indeed have had a divine origin. Without superhuman virtue, without superhuman dignity, without divine wisdom, such a design could never have been undertaken. It is difficult enough to plan for a future of ten years. That our Imperial Ancestors should have established an Empire a myriad ages since, planning well a design coeval with heaven and earth, that they should have succeeded in setting up an imperishable Dynasty, that they should have founded this sacred Empire, which will endure as long as the sun and the moon, that they were able fully to conceive and carry out such an enterprise, argues the possession of a sacred wisdom far beyond our feeble comprehension. Nor are we alone in our astonishment for the

---

[1] By many ancient authorities regarded as the chief divine Ancestor of the Imperial Family. In Dr G. Kato's recent edition of the Kogoshūi Ame-no-minakanushi-no-mikoto is referred to as "probably the highest God worshipped in the so-called primitive monotheism of Japan".

whole world regards this achievement with amazement and respect.

By cleverness and ability some have been able to make use of a generation to further their own ends. By the exhibition of courageous valour others have dominated their age. By innate wisdom some have been able to hand down good teachings and precepts to successive generations. Sages, by their own exemplary character, have taught the necessity of practising virtue. Although skilful politicians, heroic characters, highly virtuous men, and superior persons are not lacking in every age and country, nevertheless, there exist nowhere else in the wide world beings who can compare with our Imperial Ancestors, who accomplished the sacred task of establishing this imperishable Dynasty.

Is it not said that nothing comes suddenly into being at the moment it is perceived but that everything has a previous cause? There is always good reason for the prosperity and decay of national institutions. The greatness or downfall of nations is always implemented by distant causes. A great vessel requires many years of effort before it is brought to perfection. Those who would produce such a vessel must at the outset ponder many methods and give themselves to deep thought far beyond the capacity of an ordinary builder. In the same way the efforts which must be put forth by the founder of a nation are beyond the ken of ordinary mortals. Our nation which courageously maintains its Imperial integrity in the midst of its rivals upon the stage of the worldwide struggle for existence, our nation which ever increases in power and prestige, our nation which receives the willing homage of foreign peoples, is founded upon a sacred design which was conceived a myriad ages ago. Thus we who are subjects revere the divine will which brought the Empire into being, thus we serve and obey the Emperor, and hope earnestly that we shall never fail in our service. In the winter we realise that the foliage of the pine is evergreen. In the midst of storms which would rob a nation of its possessions at the slightest opportunity, in the midst of greedy avarice that never rests, surrounded by all manner of aggression which never sleeps, our Empire stands immovable. Thus when we think of the sacred virtues of our Imperial Ancestors who originated this Empire we can never cease from thankfulness, nor can we abate our reverence when we recall the divine wisdom whose keen intelligence was able to pierce the distant future and prepare the mighty design. How can we ever fail to exert ourselves to the utmost to fulfil our duties as subjects of such an Empire?

CHAPTER IX

The Inculcation of Virtue

THE relation of mankind and virtue is like the effect produced by the wind upon the grasses of the field. When the wind blows we see the grasses bending their heads. Men do not oppose the truly virtuous man, they seek rather to gain his friendship, and they defer to him as much as possible. Because virtue will make us worthy citizens we cultivate it, seek to increase our share of it, study it, and endeavour to fully realise it in our lives. All regard the possession of virtue as an ideal which they seek to attain. Although the august virtues of our Imperial Ancestors are beyond our comprehension they are none the less responsible for that flourishing condition which the Empire has exhibited from its foundation, they are responsible for that perfection of learning and culture whereby the national life is enabled to rest in a glorious tranquillity which resembles the bosom of the ocean in spring. It is due to their influence that great and small alike are characterised by the virtues of benevolence and obedience. It is due to them that the voice of envy is absent from our land.

Virtue influences the human heart and makes men obedient and submissive. If superiors are possessed of virtue inferiors, influenced by it, must inevitably revere them. If individuals would cultivate virtue and refrain from mutual contention they would be followers of the way of true humility and would realise the virtue of true submission. Under such circumstances the whole people enjoy peace and society rejoices in tranquillity. Such a society will not only be characterised by true honesty and respect for the property of others, it will actively exert itself to encourage virtue. Hence from of old those who have possessed virtue have succeeded and those who have lacked it have failed. Wisdom and courage without virtue are useless. Mere wisdom cannot prevail nor can simple courage dominate mankind. We must not too blindly rely upon wisdom and courage. Only the wisdom and courage which are combined with virtue can endow men with the true elements of success. If we make no mistake here we shall the more easily fulfil our whole duty and destiny as filial sons and true subjects.

In the days of primal chaos, before society took form, or the primitive barbarians had been brought within the domain of the Imperial Line, when lawless men flourished and laid violent hands upon Imperial possessions, Jimmu Tenno[1] appeared upon the earth. Possessed of divine valour he put forth his strength and subjugated the eastern lands. In a short time he banished the rebels, punished the evildoers, encouraged good government and culture, nourished his people, opened up the country, and established the Imperial Dynasty, thus becoming the First Ancestor of the Emperors. When we reverently search the annals concerning his accession to the Imperial Rank we learn that he established and ordained the worship of the Imperial Ancestors, that he set up the forms of government, that he exalted men of virtue, that he rewarded the meritorious, that he enshrined the three Imperial Emblems, and, in short, laid the immutable foundations of our Empire. How great his august virtue and how magnificent his Imperial Design! "Human society takes on true value with the emergence of the sage." In his immortal deeds he displayed the virtue of heaven and earth. He founded the Empire and established its immutable Dynasty on a basis wide and deep. Is not this the lesson of our early history? Is not this achievement worthy of our undying wonder and praise?

In his fourth year the Emperor Suijin[2] issued the following proclamation:

Our Imperial Ancestors condescended to take upon themselves the Imperial Office, not for their own glory but rather for the purpose of

---

[1] The Emperor Jimmu, founder of the Imperial Line in Yamato, was born, according to the ancient chronology, in B.C. 711 and died in B.C. 585. On the same authority his accession to the throne is said to have taken place in B.C. 660.

[2] B.C. 97–29.

nurturing and governing a race of gods and men. With this object they sustained the forms of government, and from time to time manifested in special acts their august virtues. We now have received and do perpetuate this sacred enterprise. We shall cherish and nourish our subjects, continue the customs of the Imperial Ancestors, and endeavour above all else to perpetuate the Imperial Dynasty. We adjure, therefore, all members of the nobility and all retainers that they fulfil the duty of loyalty, and maintain the peace of the realm.

From age to age the people have revered the Emperors and lauded their sacred virtues. Thus, upon the shores of the Pacific a mighty Dynasty has arisen, maintaining the integrity of its domains within the boundary of the seas, founding an imperishable Empire, and perpetuating an immutable Line. The whole world must recognise that such a phenomenon is not an accidental growth but a logical and natural consequence.

In my opinion the opening up of the country which followed the Meiji Restoration resulted in a sudden diversion of the tide of western civilisation to the shores of Japan which broke through and overflowed the boundaries and sanctions of our moral philosophy. Blinded by the material advantages of the new civilisation a group of superficial people arrogantly adopted the new customs and were promptly led astray. At the same time, however, there were superior people who were able to assimilate the new culture more successfully. These superior-minded elements, who interpreted aright the true spirit of the age, gave close attention to the question of popular tendencies. They carefully directed the new conceptions and habits of the people. They took care to arouse and stimulate that section of the people who, influenced by the magnificence of the material advantages of the new civilisation, were in danger of neglecting all else. The true Way for the people of Japan takes cognisance of the fact that without virtue there is no true civilisation, that without virtue there can be no true honour, and that the learning and valour which are not combined with virtue are indeed nought but barbarous valour and empty wisdom.

There are some who profess fear lest the daily advance of modern culture may mean the setting aside of moral qualities. Because there are clever people to-day who affect to despise the simple integrity of those who believe that honesty is the best policy, some men are led to believe that a man who seeks immediate profit and material advantage is a model of wisdom and ability. This is a temporary error which will not hold sway for any length of time. The culture which attracts the true subject of this Empire must be an all-round culture. Those who regard these temporary tendencies with alarm are troubling themselves unnecessarily. It goes without saying that the culture which should flourish within the bounds of this Empire is a complete and full-orbed culture. It must include an adequate conception of virtue which can produce all-round subjects and noble citizens. Our incomparable Emperor fosters such virtue among his subjects by his august qualities and by the magnitude of his Imperial Design. Truly, our Empire stands aloft in glorious isolation above the other nations of the earth, setting them a noble example.

Although voices of regret which declare that frugality is abandoned, that true humanity is disappearing, and that mankind grows ever more shallow are heard on every hand, such despondency is not justified, for the moral light of mankind really increases with the alterations of successive ages. When those who have perfected their education and cultivated their talents apply themselves to the acquisition of virtue the result is incomparably superior to the achievement of those who attempt to cultivate virtue without these other advantages. When we realise this the foolishness of such despondency must be the more apparent.[1]

There are some who teach that virtue can be separated into two sections which are designated respectively "public virtue" and "private virtue". This division is faulty. The essential principle of virtue is contained in an indivisible unity. Virtue

[1] For General Nogi's marginal comments on this passage see Appendix, paragraph 10.

is not a thing that can be separated into different departments.[1] People who would make this distinction fall into the error of imagining that there are different kinds of virtue from a contemplation of its outward manifestations or the forms in which it is expressed. The essence of virtue is an absolute unity. Despite the attempt to separate virtue into public and private virtue no man has ever been found who while seriously lacking in private virtue displays a complete and perfect public virtue. Nor is the reverse true. Virtuous people cannot be complete in one kind of virtue and lacking in the other kind. The truly virtuous man who aspires after perfection of character exhibits the virtue which he possesses both in public acts and in private life. It is unthinkable that the virtue of such a man could only be manifested in private life. We cannot but be entirely sceptical regarding the validity of this foolish argument of distinct virtues which appears from time to time.

Our Imperial Ancestors established virtue from the very foundation of the Empire. That virtue needs no completion or addition. Let the whole body of our subjects ever regard virtue as a single unit. Let them revere the sacred immutable virtue of the Emperors. Then we shall see that this faith and this doctrine which form the central conception of the Empire will advance hand in hand with our daily progress in civilisation, ever increasing in power and authority. Truly such a conception should bring us boundless joy and happiness!

[1] See Appendix, paragraph 11.

CHAPTER X

The Aspirations of the Masses

TURN the hand over and the rain falls. Turn it up and the heavens are clouded. So inconstant and variable are national policies. In what can mankind then put its trust? Men must inevitably degenerate if they suffer constant deception. Without objects of faith or trust human life is soon lost in an aimless and drifting state. Without objects of faith and trust how can there be union in loyal service to the Emperor? How can effective policies be maintained toward neighbouring countries? Such errors, however, have never characterised the subjects of this Empire. Inconstancy like that of the changing heavens has never been a characteristic of the Japanese. No matter what the intrigues that mar the policies of foreign nations we Japanese observe our treaties abroad and are ever ready to sacrifice ourselves in loyal service to the Emperor. The hearts of our people, whether we consider a thousand or ten thousand, are a unit. The same aspirations are found in each of the myriad hearts. It is an exceedingly difficult matter for a whole people to be thus united. Only among the subjects of Japan is this phenomenon to be observed. How boundless must be our joy that this is so! With this fact in mind it needs no great study to realise why the Empire of Japan, founded in the utmost antiquity, has been able to maintain a single unbroken Imperial Line. History is here provided with a unique type of Empire which from earliest times has advanced steadily and with undisturbed dignity upon the flowing tide of world civilisation.

Although a unity of the hearts of the people is good, as far as it goes, it is necessary first to see that those hearts are properly cultivated. Should the aspirations of the people degenerate this very unity may become the source of national downfall. Such has frequently been the case in the course of human history. The true aspiration is fixed on loyalty and stimulates the individual to sacrifice life itself in the service of Emperor and Empire, should the occasion arise. The true heart is manifest in perfect filial piety, in unblemished friendship, in connubial bliss, and mutual faith. Such aspirations must not only govern the lives of subjects but must unite in furthering the Imperial policies which have regard to the opening of the country to the reception of foreign civilisation. Such united aspirations must also be the basis of ethical training, and progress. Necessary as it is to plan for daily progress there must be unity in maintaining and perpetuating the glories of the past. It is the chief duty of each subject to attain such unity of aspiration. A true and well-ordered life is founded upon such aspirations. Thus the spiritual unity of the subjects of this Empire is based upon a firm and unconquerable faith, which we make our standard and objective. No matter how closely you may analyse the lives of the subjects of this Empire no exception is to be found. What cause for rejoicing there is in this thought!

According to the historical record Prince Bu of the kingdom of Gi, while floating upon the bosom of the river Sei, turned to his vassal Goki and said, "How beautiful is the treasure our country possesses in this impregnable combination of mountains and rivers!" To which Goki replied,

Our strength is in the virtue of the people and not in impregnable strongholds. Of old Prince Sambyō had Lake Dōtei on his left, and the insurmountable range of Kō Shun on his right, nevertheless, he was overthrown by Prince U. Emperor Ketsu's country was bounded on the left by rivers and on the right by the stronghold of Taika, the impenetrable mountains of Iketsu were on his south, while the passes guarded his north, nevertheless Prince Tō conquered him. Emperor Chū's territory had Mōmon on its left and Taiko on its right, mountains guarded its north and rivers bounded its south, nevertheless Bu killed him. Without virtue the people in this very boat may become your enemies.

To which Prince Bu agreed. The strength of impregnable mountains and unfordable rivers is indeed insufficient, nor is trust to be put in the power of armies. Complete reliance can only be put in the united heart of the people. With such unity we may confidently put our trust in natural defences and in the power of our arms. What are mountains and rivers and armies without unity of aspiration and purpose in the heart of the people? To overcome the defences of mountains and rivers is not the most difficult of enterprises, nor is it hard to overthrow armies. We must never forget, however, that the true aspirations of the lowliest are above price. These precious aspirations must be carefully cultivated and nourished. It is natural indeed that statesmen should exert themselves to win hearts. Once the hearts and true aspirations of the masses are united neither natural barriers nor rival armies are to be feared. To-day all civilised nations are like racehorses ranged bridle to bridle in strenuous mutual competition. National success in this contest waits upon unity of purpose in the hearts of the people. If unity of purpose in the heart of the people is strong and vigorous the nation may face a myriad foes without anxiety. The subjects of our Empire have never been lacking in this respect. May this immemorial jewel of our national glory be ever exalted in unparalleled effulgence, a lasting wonder to the startled gaze of foreign peoples.

After Kusunoki Masashige, obeying the Imperial commands, had fought the rebels at Minatogawa unsuccessfully, he entered the hut of a Kawakita peasant. Seating himself he removed his armour, revealing the eleven wounds which he had received. Turning to his companion Masasue he said, "What will happen after we are dead?" Masasue replied, "Though born into the world as human beings seven times we shall never cease from killing rebels". Smiling with pleasure Masashige said, "Your sentiments agree with mine". They then slew each other. Is this not one of the most beautiful among the many stories of those ancient days? Nevertheless, the reply of Masasue reflects more than the aspirations of his own heart. It reflects the spirit which pervades the masses of our fellow countrymen. When our Imperial people is faced with a great task the nation stands firm as a mountain and is not to be uprooted. Revering their great principles, fulfilling their obligations to the Emperor, counting neither life nor treasure before his service, the people aspire only to follow the glorious path of duty. This is verily the heart of the people. These aspirations have been manifested since the opening up of the country in the process of acquiring the elements of a new civilisation. They are displayed in the effort to achieve greater efficiency. They are displayed in the fulfilment of the great duty of maintaining the national institutions and serving the nation with life itself. There is but one thing we fear, namely, an insufficient execution of the Emperor's commands. Herein are the myriad hearts of the masses united.

Rai Sanyō[1] has written thus:

Formerly, an old gentleman of Heian (Kyōto) recounted the fact that during the Genki Era the Imperial palaces were in a tumble-down condition and that urchins entering by the broken walls disported themselves in the palace precincts, digging up the gardens in their play. With the advent of Oda Nobunaga,[2] the Imperial palaces, for the first time, became worth looking at.

Oda Nobunaga, however, is not alone in such service. Whether formerly or in the present day, unchanging from age to age, such conceptions of service have ever been the central aspirations of the people. This spirit of loyal service is something to be jealously guarded and diligently preserved. That the subjects of our Emperor have nothing to be ashamed of in this regard is one of the special glories of our country, a fact without parallel abroad. It is something truly beyond the standards of ordinary human

[1] Rai Sanyō, the famous Japanese historian and scholar, flourished in the early part of the nineteenth century. He was the author of the "Nihon Gwaishi" or "History of the Japanese People", a well-known work written in the classical style.

[2] Oda Nobunaga, the first of the great triumvirate of military leaders and statesmen of mediaeval Japan, was born in 1533 and died at the hand of one of his lieutenants in 1582. Although he began his career in 1549 with four small cantons in Owari he died master of thirty-two out of the sixty-eight provinces of Japan. It was in 1568 that he became master of Kyōto.

excellence. Year by year our population increases until it is now in the neighbourhood of fifty millions.[1] No matter how great that increase the heart of the people beats ever as one. Nothing is lacking here. The perfect fulfilment of the obligations and duties of loyalty and filial piety is the *summum bonum* of our nation. Is this not the chief glory of the people of Japan? What a happy situation this is!

From of old our subjects have been rich in such aspirations. They have been rich in the spirit of progress and advance. They have always possessed the ability to realise successive reforms with vigour. They have been efficient in maintaining the integrity of their national institutions. Through observance of the obligations of loyalty to the Emperor the spirit of patriotism has grown strong. Unity of aspirations has ever been the key-note. In order to instruct his sons Mori Motonari[2] drew attention to the alternate weakness and strength of arrows taken singly and in a bundle fastened together. Such ancient lessons, however, are quite unnecessary in this country. There is a saying that if a man is in earnest he can overcome every obstacle. The earnest purpose of a single man can drive an arrow through the toughest metal or the hardest stone, according to the proverb. There is no reason to doubt this. If that is so how much more certain is the success of a million united hearts. There is also a saying that the union of many mouths can melt the hardest metals.[3] Such a union of many minds and many mouths, such a unity in the whole nation is the dearest hope of the statesmen of any land. How difficult it is to realise is undoubtedly shown by the facts. Only in our Empire, on these eastern confines of Asia, can there be found such sustained unity of purpose. It is a union of all our hearts in honouring and exalting the virtues of learning and culture in the Emperor above.

---

[1] The population of Japan is at present (1928) approximately 78,000,000.

[2] Mori Motonari (1496–1571), a famous warrior and feudal lord who ruled wide domains in the days of Hideyoshi in the country of Sanyō, now known as Hiroshima Prefecture.

[3] For General Nogi's marginal comments on this passage see Appendix, paragraph 12.

In the subjects below it is manifested in a united desire to fulfil their high obligations. Verily, the fifty million hearts of our people are one, and the heart of each subject is the heart of all. In union the hearts of the masses exalt the prestige and honour of the nation, establishing it ever more firmly. Is not this a true description of our Empire? To unite in maintaining our reputation as true vassals of the Emperor is our highest duty.

CHAPTER XI

The Realisation of Beauty

THERE is nothing men hate more than a viper, and evil is equally distasteful. Nothing delights men more than glad tidings,[1] yet noble character is equally pleasing. Men turn aside from the evil and welcome the noble as a hundred streams seek their lower levels. Evil men become the outcasts of society while the worthy are honoured in palaces. This is but natural. In the same manner the world judges a country by its good or bad qualities. The evil nation is ostracised while a worthy people is respected and welcomed by all. How important it is to appreciate this clearly! To exclude evil and honour good, to flee from wickedness and cultivate righteousness is a necessity on earth and a command from heaven. How can a man who practises self-control live in the company of evil or remain familiar with wickedness? Although these considerations are theoretically correct, practice continues to exhibit the influence of calculations of immediate profit. Officials are prone to be too limited in their outlook. In the world many rely upon a misuse of power, or unwittingly become involved in foolish evils. While such mean men triumph wise men hide in the mountains. When vipers prevail the noble dragon withdraws. Nevertheless, such conditions are always temporary. Evil will not prevail for ever. Such misfortunes will pass away with the dissipation of the morning mist. The saying "If men are determined they may conquer heaven" does not apply to evil designs. That which we desire is the lasting honour of the nation and its august forward progress. Our people are at peace and the whole country is tranquil though we are situated in the midst of powerful rivals. We follow right undisturbed, avoiding evil, fulfilling our great duties as subjects of the Empire, achieving our high ideals, preserving those national institutions granted to us from

[1] For General Nogi's marginal comments on this passage see Appendix, paragraph 13.

of old and perpetuating them inviolate into the boundless hereafter. To accomplish this task is truly not only our great desire and hope, it is our very life. To guard this mission must be our essential duty.

When evil precepts flourish and men neglect truth, when sound opinions are not held, what shall people do to be saved? Then the world is turned upside down, wild grasses flourish, and useful plants wither. The land laments this desolation which must only end in death. Even true and righteous patriots are overcome with tears. Even benevolent sages sorrow so excessively that they wring out their sleeves in sympathy. Mischievous and perverse opinions frequently poison the mind of the people and bring chaos into society. Such nations will never succeed in encouraging true wisdom nor in stimulating to worthy endeavour the hearts of men. All who are indignant at this state of affairs should apply themselves to the cultivation of righteousness, and the acquisition of nobility. They should seek the true peace of society, and endeavour to ensure the tranquillity of the realm. In our modern world social intercourse grows more complicated with each passing year. Social changes take place more frequently with the passage of time. Humanity competes in new ways every day. It is a period in which it is very easy to fall into the bad habit of rejecting every old and established fashion. At such a time we must concentrate on eliminating what is evil and demonstrating what is true. At such a time it is essential to suppress wickedness and encourage true nobility. At such a time it is necessary to make clear the great principles upon which this Empire is founded. All mischievous teachings which do not accord with our national objectives must be ruthlessly exposed and eliminated. Our unassailable supremacy in this world is due to our vigilance in this respect. This is never to be forgotten.

Menacing clouds cut off the light of heaven. Evil teachings abound and obscure the way of true loyalty. Turbulent currents are in flood and the clear waters are overwhelmed. People run after profit and worship power. They are blinded by the attractions of popularity and have no ambition to acquire nobility of character. We do not know where this repudiation of good customs is likely to stop. Evil-minded vulgarians are found on every hand. Possessed of material prosperity they are yet ignorant of propriety. If a man stumbles they ostracise him. If a country is weak there are those who are ready to pounce upon it. These are phenomena but too familiar in the pages of history. If one house grows weak another usurps its place. If one dynasty is overthrown another takes its place. Man devours man, family struggles with family, and dynasty contends with dynasty. One nation endeavours to wrest its possessions from another nation. Have we not all seen frequent examples of this? With such floods of evil in the world where can we find a nation which does not require to cleanse its crown and its robes from evil filth? Though the world is wide and nations numerous, such a state cannot be found unless we seek it in the east. That nation is none other than our glorious Empire of Japan, which stands aloft in lonely grandeur like the white summit of Fuji. Is not this the unique phenomenon in which we glory? Our service offered to the Emperor is never for a selfish end. Is not our present prosperity due to this condition? If that true way should ever degenerate and cease to be effective, if the human heart should decay and lack the elements of regeneration, the nation must surely suffer downfall and the people destruction. The policy which will ensure the everlasting glory of the nation will also stimulate the spirit of the people and encourage the realisation of the national ideals in the daily life. Once the spirit of the people is truly stimulated and the ideals of the nation firmly established, then, though wild teachings may abound, the nation and the people are safe. None can fail to understand the reasons for the supremacy of our country. If the subjects conceive clearly the great Way of loyalty and filial piety, if they unite their aspirations here, if they realise that by achieving these noble characteristics they are indeed accomplishing the sacred will of the Emperor, they will surely thereby strengthen the firm foundation upon which the Empire stands.

Mere material progress is often the root of decay in the human heart. In the course of this type of development society experiences many sudden changes which often lead people astray. Such a situation leads to great and dangerous assaults upon human wisdom. Although, up to the present, material progress has been well employed, with the result that our culture is in a flourishing condition, nevertheless, if this material progress is ever misused good customs will be injured and miserable bloodshed may ensue. National morals will be poisoned and serious harm will be unavoidable. Since the Restoration foreign culture has poured in and overwhelmed us with the impetus of a mighty flood and the rushing current of a mountain torrent. We have withstood these assaults well, selecting and assimilating what was of value and making good use of it to our advantage. At the same time we did not throw away our native culture. We were able to achieve a parallel progress in both the material and the moral sphere. Is such a success a mere accident? The fact that our Empire has been able to conserve the dual values of its material and moral culture is due solely to the virtues of our sacred Emperor and to the united efforts of his subjects who have never failed in their loyalty.

According to the ancient tradition,

There was a woodcutter of Tōki in the Province of Mino who was remarkable for his filial piety. Although his father was fond of "sake" the son sorrowed continually because poverty prevented him from supplying it. One day, while cutting firewood in the mountains, he stumbled and fell. Whereupon he noticed a spring welling up among the rocks which greatly resembled "sake". Drinking some of the liquid from the hollow of his hand he sensed a pleasant exhilaration. Thereafter he collected the liquid daily and presented it to his father. Hearing of this incident the reigning Emperor declared that filial piety had changed the water to "sake", ordered his palanquin to be borne to the spot, and renamed the fountain the "Waterfall of Yōro".

The reverent service which the people of this Empire accord to their parents is of a similar nature. We need never doubt that where there is a will to serve there is also a way to accomplish that service. The people of this nation never tire of displaying such virtues, which are of the most ancient origin.

According to our historical records

When the fleeing Ashikaga Takauji returned with the impetus of a mighty tide to attack Kyōto, Kusunoki Masashige, obeying the commands of the Emperor, went to intercept him at Hyōgo. Although he exerted every effort to defeat the rebel he was overcome through lack of numbers and died with his younger brother Masasue. When Masashige left Kyōto he was already aware that he could not succeed. At the Sakurai post station he called his son Masatsura to him and laid upon him an injunction to continue the war against the rebels. Masatsura wept and begged to be allowed to accompany his father. Whereupon Masashige said, "I leave you behind, not for my own sake, but for the good of the country. You, however, do not comprehend, but cry like a young girl at parting. You are no son of mine ". At these words Masatsura swallowed his tears and obeyed his father's commands. He was then thirteen years old.

Not only was the father, Kusunoki, with his unique sense of loyalty, an example of chivalry which commands our utmost admiration, his son Masatsura also, when he grew to manhood, displayed ideal qualities of loyalty which we all envy and praise and long to imitate. How true it is that "the spirit of the three-year-old does not alter in the centenarian ". To offer our lives in the service of loyalty and filial piety is the true desire of every subject. That we have received from our ancestors a rich infusion of the spirit of loyalty and filial piety is also beyond question. At present, the country is flooded with the elements of material civilisation and many are blinded and led astray by these attractions. Nevertheless, with care, we shall be able to control these phenomena and direct them to profitable ends. At the same time we shall conserve the institutions that we have derived from the past. The source of success in these endeavours is to be found in the magnificent loyalty and true filial piety of the people. This essential spirit of the nation must form the basis of all true national education. That this must be the true Way of the subject must never be forgotten.

CHAPTER XII

The True Spirit of the Nation

DURING the past three thousand years innumerable nations have appeared upon the two hemispheres. Every one of these nations has had its own peculiar form of national organisation. Wherever there is a country there is found some form of government. National organisations differ with respect to the number of persons in whom are vested the powers of government. When government is vested in the hands of many we have a republic. When its prerogatives are confined to the few or even to a single person we have a totally different form of government. Thus arise many distinctions between national organisations. The government of our Empire is Imperial in form. The august prerogatives of government in this land repose in the person of a unique and sacred Emperor who rules enthroned above. Below, a whole nation looks up to him with reverent awe and serving him fears nothing so much as some dereliction in that service. The beauty of this complementary virtue, which is the very basis of our Empire and which grows ever more transcendent and more firmly established, has endured unchanged from the utmost antiquity. It is but natural that each nation should have its own peculiar institutions. What then are the peculiar national institutions of our Empire? They are indeed well known to us. We always regard them with pride and do our utmost to demonstrate their peculiar beauties to the whole world.

National institutions inevitably have aspects which are to be commended and others which are to be condemned. Sometimes powerful families exert their strength arrogantly. Again, a powerful and tyrannical ruler may appear upon the throne. Violence may call forth violence and strength contend with strength. Cruelty and oppression may go hand in hand. Foreign countries have ever sought in vain to realise a perpetual peace. The reason for this state of affairs is that in these foreign countries the apparently superior persons are not really superior, and the same is true of their inferiors. Even insignificant men are able to seize power and prevail over their fellows. By an opportune usurpation of power they may even command the homage due to true rulers. They may even aspire to the throne. But let their oppressive rule slacken for a moment and innumerable rivals spring up and battle for the possession of the country. There are countless instances of this character in the annals of foreign nations. We need never doubt this fact for a moment. Such phenomena are natural. They arise from deficiencies or faults in the national organisation. We cannot afford to neglect these national institutions which give rise to such phenomena as are displayed in world history. There are, however, certain phenomena unique and unparalleled in the history of other nations, whose glory still shines brightly after a myriad ages. Such are to be witnessed only in our Empire. Our superior national institutions are not comparable with those of other nations. Indeed, in the history of our Empire there has never appeared a single usurper, a rebel, or a calumniator of the throne. None has ever complained of oppression. In peaceful content the whole people has basked from time immemorial as though in the gentle breezes of spring. Our lives and our hearts are ever at one with the will of our Emperor. This constant unity is the peculiar glory of our nation and constitutes the essential principle and the true spirit of our national institutions. Oh, how happy we are in the possession of this unique spirit which from the most ancient times has never been paralleled in human history.

Loyalty is the source of all virtues and of all good. To realise this highest of virtues is the true aspiration of every subject. Those who apply themselves to their various occupations, those who toil ceaselessly at their trades think only of the prosperity and well-being of their country. Whether our statesmen go abroad to conduct the diplomatic affairs of their country or remain at home to direct the business of government, whether they concern themselves with military or civil affairs, they seek always to keep pace with the progress of the rest of the world. Should national emergencies arise our people are ever ready to sacrifice their lives in courageous and loyal service. Such, indeed, is the true spirit of our forty million compatriots. This spirit has been the sure and unique possession of our people since that remote antiquity wherein our nation was established. Such self-forgetful service, such a peerless service constitutes our most precious adornment and is without parallel in the annals of other nations. To such an ideal of loyalty do the myriad subjects of this nation aspire. Each and every one endeavours to achieve the object of this aspiration. Even in the least detail of their lives they seek to avoid any dereliction in the performance of the duties of loyalty. Serving their parents our people seek to be truly filial; towards their brothers they endeavour to be fraternal. In the home peaceful connubial relations are their ideal. Towards their friends they endeavour to maintain the relation of trust. They emulate each other in observing the duties of mutual respect and the love of humanity. Furthermore, they endeavour to keep pace with the most progressive elements in world society. Realising clearly the needs of their nation they devote themselves to the repayment of that grace of which they have been the recipients. These are the duties which our people acknowledge. According to the ancient saying, "As the dying leopard leaves its fur to grace posterity so a man's reputation remains after his death". Our Imperial people aspire to leave such a reputation that dying they may bequeath the fame of a sacrificial loyalty. To accomplish and to revere the virtue of loyalty is our inviolable and loftiest aspiration and the central ideal of Nippon Shindo.

From our parents we have received our physical being. Our fathers with discipline and our mothers with affection have nourished and reared us and made us what we are. This is a natural order. We for our part must to the utmost of our strength devote ourselves to the filial service of our fathers and our mothers. Thus shall we repay their care. This relation is an indissoluble one. To the wrath of our fathers and our mothers we must meekly submit and in patience await the cooling of their anger. Instant obedience to the commands of our parents and a service which neither fire nor flood can hinder are peculiar beauties of our national character. No matter what alterations may take place in the world of thought, no matter what confusions and changes may arise in the material sphere, parents must always remain parents and children children, in respect to the obligations of filial piety. The immutable sanctions of filial piety have never been departed from nor has the connubial accord of our homes been disturbed for a thousand epochs, or seniority in the family group assailed. Such are the true ideals of filial piety which have been handed down through successive generations from the remotest antiquity. Thus filial piety also arises from the desire to fulfil the whole duty of loyalty. It is said that, "The final object of filial piety is to honour our parents". It is due to the obligations of loyalty that we diligently seek day by day to observe the duties of filial piety. It is due to this primary obligation that we seek ever to fulfil our duties to our parents endeavouring by our efforts to bring honour rather than shame upon our elders. Governed by such motives we do not seek even to escape those obligations which would leave our dead bodies upon foreign shores or force us to endure excruciating sufferings. We fear only our own defects and insufficiencies in this service. Such are the sentiments of true loyalty. Parents also are parents and children children. The relation between them is close and intimate and mutual affection is strong. These are the phenomena which contribute to the living history of our Empire.

Each country has its own peculiar characteristics. The safety or peril of the nation is closely related to the spirit which it cherishes. Upon that spirit may depend the glorious prosperity or the decline of the nation. The progress or regression of the state, peace or turmoil among the individual citizens, all are conditioned by the essential spirit of the national institutions. Examples of the consequence of this dependence may be met with frequently in the history of nations. Such phenomena are also certain to be repeated in the future. In accordance with the spirit of our peculiar national institutions, however, our people have ever served the Emperor with consistent loyalty and their parents with filial piety, never neglecting either obligation. Applying itself to the diligent practice of trade or calling, endeavouring to cast shame neither on nation nor on parents this people has endured to the present. From the foundations of the world two suns have never shone in the heavens nor shall two suns ever shine therein while heaven endures throughout its countless myriad epochs. In like manner our people shall never revere two Emperors nor even conceive the idea of a second ruler. Without doubt this spirit of our people shall endure for a thousand myriad epochs, and never cease. It is said that even crows have sufficient filial affection to repay the care of the parent birds. How much more then should man possess the sentiment of this service! As we have seen, this benevolent spirit is especially warm in the bosoms of our people. The country is full of such loyal and filial citizens. How hopeful is the future of our Empire! How happy and glorious is our destiny! This essential spirit of our national institutions must indeed endure coeval with the Empire. By means of this spirit its basis shall be for ever secure. The flower and fruit of that spirit shall flourish in glorious abundance. The aspirations of our Imperial people are well reflected in the poem: "Should men enquire of the Yamato spirit of Japan their answer shall be the wild mountain cherry blossom fragrant in the morning sun".

The loftiest aspiration and the supreme endeavour of the citizen of this Empire is to fulfil the twin obligations of loyalty and filial piety.

CHAPTER XIII

The Basis of Education

FORTY years ago our Empire at a single stroke abandoned the ancient culture of the East and took its place upon the swift current of modern civilisation. Education became essential and soon flourished in every part of the land. It became the most important means of guiding and directing our lives. Without it we were not able to enter good society. Wealth and birth alone without education were found to be insufficient. Without distinction of rank or wealth, therefore, all the citizens of the Empire devoted themselves with the utmost diligence to the cultivation of learning and the acquisition of an education. By this means they demonstrated their single-hearted devotion to the Imperial Line. Such devotion is the glory of our ancestral tradition and the true adornment of the present age.

The purpose of education is to provide nurture for men of character. This cultivation has a two-fold object. One kind of education is designed to produce the great leader, the man of all time. The other kind is for the purpose of producing the man adapted to the requirements of the age.[1] When education realises this dual objective it is successful. In order to produce his superman the educator must not consider the achievements of any one nation, he must not be swayed by international rivalries. He must consider neither merit nor renown, neither the handful of rice nor the gourd of wine. He must concentrate on producing the man who will be great for all time. His task is to produce material which will ensure the permanent peace and prosperity of the nation. The second great object of education is to produce men who are suited to the changing times and who are able to adapt themselves with ease to the immediate emergency. By producing people who are thus adaptable educators will enable the citizens to fulfil their duties to the nation.

[1] For General Nogi's marginal comments on this passage see Appendix, paragraph 14.

Our Empire is not limited to any ephemeral existence. It will achieve an immortal and everlasting destiny. It must possess in its history the elements of both permanent and temporary existence. Educators must not fail to adapt their methods to this end. To ensure both present and future prosperity they must carefully nourish and produce such men as will secure the true progress of the Empire and who will be trained at the same time to take advantage of the changing conditions in the world. I have designated one type of education immediate or practical education and the other potential or ideal education. I consider these two types of education to be essential to the maintenance of a flourishing and peaceful Empire. The direction of education with a view to producing either the superman or the practical man, the choice of practical or ideal methods must be left to the wise leadership of our educators. They must be careful in their choice. At the same time those who receive their instruction must consider their own capacities in order to choose aright between the two alternative types of education available. If care is taken in making suitable choice then although the paths of ascent are different all may unite in admiration of the view from the summit, and the merit of their several efforts shall be of equal value. All will rank as equals for they must all be regarded as equally fulfilling their full duties as subjects.

Education for the most part has its home in the schools. This is natural. Schools great and small have been established for this purpose. They increase in number daily and there is no limit to this expansion. The progress and dissemination of education is indeed wonderful. Nevertheless, although schools have been established for the purpose of providing education, it is superficial to say that education is limited to the interior of the schoolroom. True education is to be found in the home, in the school, and in society. We must not forget that education is found in these three departments of life. Mōbo's[1] teaching

---

[1] The mother of Mencius. Desiring to make a scholar of her son she first took up her residence in the midst of a great city. Imitating the activities of his daily environment the infant Mencius soon began to play with the abacus. Deploring this tendency the mother hurriedly moved to the neighbourhood

of the three removals indicates the importance of the relation between education and society. The adage which declares that the spirit of the three-year-old remains unchanged for a hundred summers indicates the wonderful importance of the influence of the home. It is unfortunate that at the present time education is too much relegated to the schoolroom and the place of the home and society correspondingly disregarded. This is the most characteristic defect in educational circles. It is the duty of all true educators to cure this disease. They should not devote themselves too exclusively to the school. They should carefully consider the home and the influences of society and thus increase the effectiveness of their education.[1] The education which depends solely upon the school is a half-paralysed education and the result will be but half of what is aimed at. Those who are charged with the task of education in this Empire cannot too carefully attend to these matters nor too greatly exaggerate their care in this respect.

Through following in the footsteps of occidental nations and vigorously entering the sphere of western culture our Empire has enjoyed increased prestige and renown. Emerging from her period of immaturity her present intellectual and material achievements are inferior in no way to those of foreign nations. To maintain their present rank among foreign peoples and to sustain for ever undiminished their glorious heritage is the true task of the citizens of the Empire. The fulfilment of this mission calls for the provision of an education which is both ideal and practical, both temporary and enduring in character. To perceive these points with clarity is to see penetratingly into the future. To fulfil this mission is the true task of the citizens of the Empire. To perform these tasks is to offer true service

of a temple. Here, however, the lad soon began to imitate the unintelligent droning of the Kyōmon (Buddhist scriptures) by the priests. Dissatisfied with this the mother moved once again to the vicinity of a school. Here the small boy quickly acquired a fondness for reading while listening to the pupils who were committing the classics to memory. Thus the choice of the right environment produced the great scholar.

[1] For General Nogi's marginal comments on this passage see Appendix, paragraph 15.

to the Emperor above and to fulfil our obligations to our ancestors.

With the progress of culture national morality is perfected. True culture, indeed, must include true morality. Wisdom without virtue falls into foolish pride on the one hand or profligacy on the other. The very machinery of progress may become the means of disseminating the germs of immorality.[1] These dangers which paralyse the moral sense and cause it to degenerate, these dangers which hinder its true development must be kept carefully in mind. The new civilisation of our Empire has developed suddenly. At one leap we have entered the world of modern culture. Under such circumstances the virus of evil is, unfortunately, very strong. Perceiving this patriotic citizens cannot fail to be moved with indignation. A fervent desire to arouse and stimulate the moral sense of the nation is not limited to the national leaders. The attitude of self-righteousness cannot be permitted in any citizen. To clarify the turbid current, to destroy the bacilli of evil tendencies, to secure an adequate and balanced education for the nation must be the chief concern of every true citizen. "Without mounting its rivers to their sources who can comprehend the Konron?"[2] Those who do not comprehend the true source of our national education are in danger of becoming slaves of mere learning or of their own talents. They will not escape reproach. The true source of our national education is in the observance of loyalty and filial piety. On the one hand our fellow citizens devote themselves to the Glorious Effulgence above and on the other they serve their elders with acceptable devotion. To secure the fulfilment of these obligations is the purpose of education. There can be no other. Should there appear individuals who seem unable to conceive of the Konron they should be the special care

[1] For General Nogi's marginal comments on this passage see Appendix, paragraph 16.

[2] A saying from the Chinese classics. The Konron is a mountain range of China famous for the beauty of its scenery. In other words, unless we mount the rivers of the Konron range to their sources in the peaks we can never truly comprehend the beauty of the scenery.

of educators. We must never be lacking in devotion to our duties.

I should like to recall an incident in the ancient records by referring to a passage in Raisanyo's "History of Japan".

Shigemori spoke as follows: "It is commonly said that there are four types of benevolence in this world. Among them the benevolence of the Emperor is first. It is true that our family though originally descendants of the Emperor Kanmu Kuzuhara eventually became subjects. They became unimportant people. Even the Taira Shōgun was nothing more than a provincial governor. When Tadamori was raised to the rank of a courtier of the inner precincts there was much heart-burning because he was thought to have progressed too far. But in your case, my father, have you not reached the lofty rank of prime minister? As to even my insignificant self I have been considered worthy to be made a minister and a general. Now the Taira family are all officials in the Imperial service. Our lands cover half the country. We have been the recipients of too much gracious condescension. Who can say that it is unreasonable that other courtiers should grow to hate us? Nevertheless, our good fortune has not forsaken us and all the rebels have been thrown into prison. Confine yourself to estimating the charges to be preferred against them and leave their punishment to the Emperor. They will be deprived of their honours as a natural consequence. There is no need for hasty or violent action. I have heard it said that in our pre-occupation with the Imperial service we should neglect all private interest. We should never allow private interest to interfere with our obligations to the Emperor. Is it not easy to distinguish between the worthy and the unworthy course in this instance? I, Shigemori, have been raised from the sixth to the princely third rank. I have been overwhelmed by Imperial favours. It is clear to which party I should join myself. There are also more than two hundred samurai ready to give their lives for me, Shigemori. During the wars of the Hōgen period Yoshitomo, at the command of the Emperor, slew his father Rokujō Hangan. I thought at that time that it was an unspeakably inhuman deed. Were you not a spectator of that deed? To be loyal I must be unfilial. If I am filial I must be disloyal. I, Shigemori, am greatly troubled as to which way I should turn. Would it not be better for me to die than to live in the presence of this dishonour. If you intend to carry out the present design then do so after cutting off my head ". Thus spoke Shigemori with tears while all who were present wept with him. Kiyomori replied, "That I should undertake such deeds in my old age is not for my own benefit but for the sake of my descendants. If you consider what I do to be incorrect follow your course ".[1]

Thus did Taira Shigemori oppose the violence of his father Kiyomori who regarded neither the Imperial Throne nor the Imperial Rule. This is a beautiful tale in which are displayed the essential principles of loyalty and filial piety. This is a record which should be repeated daily and never neglected. We must not lose ourselves in a mere superficial admiration of Shigemori nor waste our effort in mechanical repetition. We must achieve a practical application of the essential principles in the example here set for us.

Filial piety is involved in loyalty and is never opposed or contrary to it. I have already explained that there is no kind of filial piety which is incompatible with loyalty. In this connection

[1] The story of these times is full of incidents of unusual political and romantic interest. The epoch marks a definite advance in Japanese feudalism paralleling the downfall of the noble house of Fujiwara in which the great champion of the military house of Taira had no small hand. Taira Kiyomori (1118-1181) was the blunt and vigorous soldier par excellence. Shigemori, his son, although undoubtedly a military leader of no mean ability was made of finer stuff. In a rough and martial age he sought to act in accordance with lofty moral ideals which frequently brought him into conflict with his father. In the present instance Shigemori is pleading for lenient treatment of the Shishigadani conspirators. This famous conspiracy (1179) of the Fujiwara family, with which the retired Emperor Go-Shirakawa seems to have been in sympathy, was undoubtedly meant to contrive the downfall of the Taira. As Shigemori points out in the course of his remonstrance it was but natural that the Fujiwara officials should be deeply chagrined at the honours heaped upon what they conceived to be a family of military upstarts. It was, of course, the attitude of the retired Emperor which complicated the situation for Shigemori. For him the obligations of loyalty to the Emperor conflicted with the claims of filial piety. This famous incident has become a classic example of the ancient controversy between the two virtues. The situation is still further complicated when it is recalled that the Emperor Antoku, who ascended the throne shortly after the suppression of the conspiracy, was the grandson of Kiyomori.

the reader is referred to the chapters on Loyalty and Filial Piety.[1]

Recently our Empire has joined hands with the other powers. She now stands among them as an equal. Academic culture flourishes on every hand and advances with the irresistible progress of the rising sun. Schools multiply upon the land like swarming bees and the subjects studied are many and various, nevertheless all these activities without exception unite in a single goal. From of old our people have been employed in a great variety of activities but their aspiration has ever been single. Throughout all ages loyalty and filial piety have remained the same. Upon this beautiful aspect of our history we may well pride ourselves. Situated in the midst of many nations we invite and welcome their culture to our shores. Standing upon a basis of equality with the great powers our country takes her part in the counsels of the world. Such considerations redound to the honour of our Empire. Such a consummation is due to the devotion of our citizens to loyalty and to their fulfilment of the obligations of filial piety. The citizens of this Empire are united in a firm determination never to neglect the least detail of the Imperial will, and they are equally resolved to demonstrate the virtue of this devotion to the whole world. They shall ever maintain inviolate the power of the people of Yamato. Such are the duties and obligations of our people.

[1] These references, included in the original in the form of a quotation, are not exact reproductions of the earlier passages. They are rather in the nature of brief summaries and correspond perhaps most closely with the sentiments expressed on pages 48 and 49.

CHAPTER XIV

The Fraternal Relation

HOW many millions of human beings are congregated upon this earth! Although each has his place and all co-operate peacefully with one another yet the closest ties are those which unite brother to brother. Brothers are of the same flesh and blood. They derive their existence from the same parents and have at least a common father or a common mother. At home brothers are the strength of families and abroad they are the source of prosperity in the nation. Therefore, from ancient times a fraternal spirit between brothers has been enforced as one of the most important of the moral precepts. I in common with others desire to make it one of the most important elements in Nippon Shindo. There is a saying that, "As brothers are prone to drift apart mankind must not put too much confidence in this natural relation". Although this may be true it does not affect the moral teaching of the fraternal relation. By brotherhood in the family humanity prospers. Humanity should, therefore, remember this obligation and this flesh and blood relation and cultivate peaceful co-operation. The true fraternal relation is the basis of national prosperity and power. In our country where family spirit is especially prominent it is no exaggeration to say that the fraternal spirit which exists between brothers is the basis of our national prosperity. Of recent years many elements of foreign civilisations have been imported. Many of our laws are modelled on various foreign legal systems. Constitutional government has been adopted as a principle. The interest of the individual has been carefully considered and the problem of national expansion studied. The rights of the individual have not been lost sight of in the effort to keep pace with world progress. Although we are the younger brother in the family of nations yet from the standpoint of legal institutions we are not behind our elder brothers. The younger brother has emerged from the seclusion of the shadows and has taken his place in the sunlight by the side of his elder brother. In our modern world even a younger brother may by his gifts of learning and his talents obtain great merit. If there should be a younger brother superior in culture and talents to his elder brother he need not always remain in submissive seclusion in the shadows. In respect to morals, however, the younger brother is always the younger brother and the older brother is ever the older brother. There can be no occasion for the disobedience of the younger brother. The younger brother must always submit to his elder brother. Between brothers the true fraternal relation must always be highly honoured. The elder brother should cherish the younger and help him to advance. The younger brother should respect and honour his elder brother. No disagreement or separation should be permitted to arise between them. Brothers should mutually support each other in obedience and love. As a result the nation will enjoy peace and true prosperity. The maintenance of the true fraternal spirit can never be lightly regarded.

That brothers must never quarrel with one another is not merely a precept of moral teaching. From practical considerations of peace and good government it is essential to enforce this teaching in the training of brothers. Should brothers engage in controversy others will come to despise them. Through the scorn of others both brothers will inevitably suffer loss. Should elder brothers hate their younger brothers or younger brothers seek to injure their elder brothers we may witness the mutual destruction of blood relations. Such untoward possibilities are to be carefully avoided by men of good judgement. We have only to rely on the cultivation of the fraternal spirit to avoid and forestall such evils. The cultivation of the fraternal relation will ensure happy co-operation between brothers. If the two elements of the fraternal relation are properly guarded true strength will accrue to the nation. If brothers fall out they not only injure themselves and destroy their families, they also bring disaster upon the state. Ceaseless care is necessary to maintain the true fraternal relation. To guide the younger and obey the elder are natural instincts. In the development of these instincts brothers mutually aid each other in establishing the true fraternal relation, their families prosper and the nation grows more powerful. This result is inevitable. This fraternal spirit arises from an instinctive emotion and its cultivation is one of the chief elements in fulfilling our obligations to the nation and in realising the ideal of loyalty to the Emperor. Those who love their country, their family, and their own well-being must regard the cultivation of the true fraternal relation as the central obligation of the citizen and devote their strength to realising this ideal in practice.

This fraternal relation is an innate and constant element which cannot be eliminated from the social order without disaster. This relation which is expressed in fraternal love, mutual helpfulness, encouragement and exhortation among those who are brothers is a source of true service to the Empire. Those who disregard this unalterable moral discipline, those who would neglect these innate bonds, those who would disobey the dictates of Nippon Shindo are not only disloyal to our Emperor, their fault can never be condoned by heaven or earth. Although it may be said that the people of Yamato do not fall into these errors they can never afford to neglect the development of this instinctive fraternal spirit. We must realise that it is the essential duty of the people of Yamato to achieve a practical realisation of this virtue.

Speaking generally, of course, all the people in the world are brothers. From the standpoint of natural phenomena all men are brothers. There should be no distinction between black and white. It is even unnecessary to regard the people of Yamato as a race apart. All men are brothers in essence although they may have different cultures. No narrow discrimination should be set up between them. If all men observed the obligations of the relation between elder and younger, if the elder would universally aid and direct the younger and the younger render due obedience, then indeed there would be no more occasion to forge the sword among men. Throughout the world the clamour of warriors and the turmoil of war would vanish and deep peace would reign in heaven and in earth. My purpose in recommending Nippon Shindo is to strengthen the bonds that exist between blood relations among the people of Yamato. Yet I do not in any way exclude the broader aspect of this relation. I believe that both aspects of the teaching are really one in their effect. I believe that to strengthen the fraternal spirit between brothers in the narrow national sense is also to further the ideal of world brotherhood. I desire to recommend this wider conception of brotherhood and increase the vitality of its claims. I desire to bring about the successful realisation of both aims. Nevertheless, for the people of this Empire I believe that the maintenance of the fraternal relation between blood brothers is an essential thing which cannot be neglected with safety for a single moment.

According to the ancient records there was once a noble of north China named Sokeinan who became Lord of Seika. At the time of his accession there lived in that country a family of farmers known by the name of Fumei. For many years the Fumei brothers had disputed about their lands until a hundred persons had become involved. Kei called the brothers to him and admonished them as follows: "It is only with tears and great efforts that men secure good brothers, but fields are easy to obtain. What does it profit you to get possession of fields if you thereby lose brothers?" All who heard the appeal were deeply moved. The Fumei brothers bowing low declared that they would reconsider the matter. The quarrel which had lasted for ten years was thus brought to a speedy end and all misunderstandings melted away. The two brothers went home together and lived in peace and harmony ever after. This tale deserves a place in the memory of men for its beauty. The bonds that bind brothers can never be rent asunder with impunity. Citizens of this land of Japan who have received the boon of life and who have been vouchsafed the benevolent grace of their Emperor must fulfil these obligations of the fraternal relation. They must realise the full significance of this normal, innate

relationship which derives from consanguinity. By such fulfilment they may set up a sure foundation for the precious institutions of home and nation, and fulfil their obligation to their
Emperor. If the elder brother truly cherishes and guides the
younger and if the younger brother obeys and follows the
instruction of the elder the obligations of the fraternal relation
are completely fulfilled. Thus do we become worthy subjects of
the Emperor. How essential is it that every citizen should
determine to perpetuate and maintain this precious fraternal
relation!

CHAPTER XV

Connubial Accord

CONNUBIAL accord is the peaceful and seemly relation in the home. It is also the foundation of peace in the nation. It is basic to the great principles of morality. National integrity rests upon it. Unless connubial accord is first established within the home it would be as useless to attempt to maintain correct morals or foster national prosperity as it would be foolish to turn the shafts to the west when we desire to journey to the east, or to angle for fish in the top of a tree. The decadent manners and customs of Gyōka and Kōdai[1] rapidly corrupted the people. Conditions in the modern age also tend to distract and pervert women old and young and entice them into evil habits. Such tendencies are apparent to-day. Led astray by them they frequently forget the true nature of their duty. Depending upon powerful and wealthy men they flaunt their arrogance in the face of society. Like a tiger freed in its native haunts or a bird released from a cage they joyously disport themselves and act in a wholly self-centred and inconsiderate manner. Unrestrained by common-sense they act like demented persons. Such lamentable tendencies are all too common. This is the inevitable detriment which accompanies a rapid development of new culture. Nevertheless, is it not our plain duty to restrict this loss as far as may be? With the growing complexities of modern society each individual life becomes more difficult and complicated. Furthermore, each country has its own peculiar nationality and its citizens their predilections. In like manner men and women differ widely in ability and capacity. Masculine talent is manifested in efficiency, courage, and determination. Feminine gifts are revealed in humility, endurance, and submission. The two parties by union and mutual support produce the true connubial relation. Thus they

---

[1] The epochs of Gyōka and Kōdai are proverbial in Chinese history for the decay of good customs and the decline of public morality.

give birth to their thousands and establish firmly their family organisations. Upon this basis also is the nation established. Thus do they set up their happy homes and achieve an ideal existence. In such service to the state and in such contribution to the welfare of society both masculine and feminine qualities must be regarded as of equal importance and as inseparable. Each party must devote itself to cultivating natural gifts and talents. Each must avoid infringement of the other's proper sphere. Strenuous competition between the sexes is injurious to the best interests of society. It is destructive to the social order and becomes the origin of dissension in the family. There is no greater misfortune in the world than this.

The culture of the Meiji era was of a remarkably broad and popular nature. The education of women outside the home was greatly developed. Feminine culture progressed and became the recognised thing. Nevertheless, though excellent results were no doubt obtained by this new movement there were also serious defects. How true it is that those who wish to make forward progress must have sufficient wisdom to avoid any consequent evils. There are too many in this world who keep their eyes upon what is immediately profitable and fail to recognise the loss involved. How remarkable this is. As there is but one supreme authority there cannot be two Emperors in the land. It is equally self-evident that there cannot be two heads to a family. This is especially obvious in our country. Indeed the duties of the two sexes are plain and require no laboured description. Nevertheless, should we confine ourselves to the superficial aspects of civilisation and neglect to produce noble wives and cultured sisters, should we fail to enforce chastity or cause the characteristic feminine virtues to shine we shall never escape grave disasters.

Men and women are as dependent upon each other as the object and its shadow. The two natures of man and woman must have a parallel existence. The development of one sex to the exclusion of the other cannot be permitted. Those who desire the eternal prosperity of heaven must endeavour to perfect the terrestrial world.[1] There must never be emphasis upon the one to the detriment of the other. Should the interests of the two be permitted to conflict the pillars of heaven will be cast down and the foundations of the earth overturned. If husband and wife cannot live peacefully together the family is destroyed and the nation injured. Under such circumstances the social order cannot but be disturbed.

Connubial accord is an ornament which adorns the state. It is a basic principle of social morality, and the foundation upon which the nation must be established. In this country, the influx of western culture since the Meiji Restoration has had a profound influence upon feminine nature. It is possible that in some respects the reaction may have been too extensive. Those who wish to profit by this culture must have sufficient wisdom to avoid its dangers. Because of inattention to this point there is a real danger that female learning may be advanced at the expense of female virtue. It is indeed unfortunate that women are taking their place in society who have theoretical knowledge but who are totally ignorant of household duties. Now that we have reached a point at which we should pause and take stock it behoves our leaders to give most careful attention to these problems. As I have reflected elsewhere regarding present conditions and tendencies,

Should there arise many painters who in their attempt to paint tigers only succeed in portraying the likeness of cats, and should they still be convinced that they have produced the likeness of a tiger, then the enlightened must needs laugh them to scorn for their foolishness, but the common people will come to the conclusion that a tiger is something which cannot be painted successfully. If many people in trying to straighten the crooked horns of cattle only succeed in killing them and then declare that the cattle died on account of their

---

[1] This is an allusion to the classic apposition of Yang and Yin or Yō and In, to give the Japanese form. In the ancient Chinese classic of Eki Heaven (Yang) represents the male principle and Earth (Yin) the female principle. It was in the seventeenth century that these doctrines, derived from the philosophical teachings of Ch'eng and Chu (known as Tei-shu in Japan) of the great Sung Dynasty, became familiar to the Japanese.

own weakness the enlightened will not be able to withhold their derision but the masses are apt to consider that there is no means of straightening crooked horns. I cannot withhold my indignation when I consider how many there are in this world who, though lacking in the necessary skill, yet endeavour to paint the tiger and straighten the horns of cattle. It was thus in the case of the demand for female education, when the country was first flooded with foreign culture at the Restoration. The necessity for feminine education no one denies. Feminine education must not be neglected for a single day. Nevertheless, should those who are responsible for this education be unacquainted with the true end of female education, should they not understand the true method of educating women then all their efforts are bound to end in failure. How important it is for them to proceed with extreme caution! I think that women must be equally respected with men but not granted the same rights, that women should be made equally wise but not accorded the same learning. I think this is the true key to the problem of female education. Those feminine educators who would grant women the same rights and the same learning as men are on a par with those who in the realm of art try to paint tigers with insufficient skill or in the realm of crafts endeavour to straighten horns without knowledge. We must reject such methods as hindering rather than advancing the cause of true feminine education.

The customs of Gyōka are not to be highly regarded nor should we be stained with the dye of Kōdai. The wife should observe the commands of her husband. The beauties of connubial harmony are to be nourished with care. Peaceful and true homes are to be produced and national prosperity thereby secured. By such means shall the nation repay the august grace of the Emperor and ensure the continued prosperity of its descendants. Thus shall its people secure the everlasting prosperity of the Empire of Japan. Thus will they realise the true fruition of their peculiar talents. Is not this the peculiar responsibility of our educators?

Heaven donates and earth bears. Heaven enfolds and earth contains. Hence all created things develop and evolve. This is the great design of creation. The stern righteousness of the husband and the true obedience of the wife uniting in mutual government of the home are modelled upon the great design of heaven and earth. This is the origin both of true domestic felicity and national prosperity. There is no falsity in the claim that the strength and prosperity of the nation depend upon the peaceful and obedient home. To say that the essential elements of peace and good government depend upon the establishment of a wholesome home life is no idle dream.

As in the heavens the sun is not double so on earth there exists but one Emperor. Two contending rulers are the certain source of national downfall. In our country, during the two thousand five hundred years that have elapsed since the age of the gods, our sacred Emperor has ruled in unimpaired dignity ceaselessly revered by his devoted subjects. The four classes have ever submitted to him and obeyed him as his children. Hence unadorned obedience and true patriotism have always been cultivated, while throughout the whole period the beauties exhibited by peaceful homes have been evident on every hand. Contemporaneously have the true virtues of loyalty and patriotism been wrought out in the courageous valour of the people. The commands of husbands and the obedience of wives are good customs not transitory in nature. They are the fundamental principles by which true Japanese homes are established, and the Emperor fitly served. Aroused as we have been from the peaceful dream of the past, new learning from the occident has successfully encroached on the old and the present culture of the Meiji era is an amalgamation of these two cultures. Some of the effects of this amalgamation are astonishing. The gentle feminine virtues have been laid aside and the vigorous manners of men imitated. Having discarded the "Onna Daigaku"[1] girl students boldly theorise about love, and without giving thought

---

[1] "The Great Learning for Women", a work of great importance in the early education of Japanese women, generally ascribed to the scholarly and virtuous wife of Kaibara Ekiken, although opinions differ as to the authorship, some holding it to be the work of the latter. See also note on Ekiken, page 103.

to the cultivation of feminine virtues indulge in unrestrained social intercourse. This situation is due to new ideas imported from abroad. We must take great care that in this reaction we are not led utterly astray from the true Way and the pure teaching. At one stride our country has become one of the five great powers. We as well as they press forward in the lists of civilisation. Under such circumstances it may be unreasonable to expect that women should be satisfied to continue the wearing of old-fashioned clothes or to restrict themselves to the practice of the ancient customs. Nevertheless, for them to turn completely aside from the customary way and to adopt entirely new manners is by no means auspicious for the future of home, nation, or social order. Women and men are related as the shadow and the substance. Women cannot exist alone nor should men be alone. Men and women uniting as husband and wife together set up the home, form the basis of the nation, secure the seemly felicity of human existence, and thus fulfil the wonderful and providential design of nature. The rights of men are fixed and separate by nature. Upon the right delimitation of these two spheres depends the establishment of the ideal home, the true national life, and a healthy state of society. I cannot agree to the unbalanced arguments of those who would assign absolute rights to men, nor yet of those who unreasonably favour women. When men and women unite to form homes the mutual interplay of their rights and interests and all their social relations will undergo variation with the ebb and flow of social life. The way to have no regrets is to avoid on the one hand the danger of being stampeded by new developments and on the other the obstinately conservative attitude, and at the same time to adapt one's self to changing conditions with skilful foresight. This is the supreme duty of the people of this country.

A happy and orderly mutual relation between husband and wife is of the essence of our national institutions and the foundation of our prosperity. That the husband should command and the wife submit, thus establishing the wholesome home and forming the healthy constituents of the nation, is the true teaching which our people can never afford to neglect. To allow themselves to be led astray in reaction from the violent changes which are taking place in society, to neglect their natural duties, to disregard the good customs of the family and thereby bring about the destruction of the constituent elements of the national life are mistakes which must be avoided at all cost by the citizens of this Empire.

The vigorous and unimpeded advance of our culture, the constant increment of our wealth and power, our supremacy in the east, our equality with the other great powers, our imposing part upon the stage of human affairs all depend upon the establishment of a healthy home life wherein husband determines and wife acquiesces. The everlasting praise of our August Ruler, the reverent service of our unique Imperial House, coeval with heaven and earth, and the enduring guarantee of truly loyal subjects all depend upon the maintenance of this true and ideal relation in the home life of the nation.

CHAPTER XVI

The Mutual Faith of Friends

HEAVEN has given birth to a myriad peoples who have multiplied exceedingly until upon the two hemispheres there are countless millions of human beings. Born though they are upon this same earth their nationalities are many and diverse. With the development of nations and peoples language and customs have become differentiated. There does not exist among them that mutual sympathy which is found within the confines of the same family. There does not exist that relation derived from similarity of descent or culture. Nevertheless, although blood relationships do not exist between the different peoples there is a certain mutual sympathy and a sentiment which unites all men and results in that virtue known as friendship. Is not the beauty of mutual trust the outstanding virtue of human beings?

Mankind does not welcome nor seek a solitary existence. Out of this fact arise the virtues which adorn humanity. Mutual friendship derives from this source. This mutual trust between friends is one of the five fundamental relations of human society. We are taught that it is never to be regarded lightly. Out of faith arises the true sentiment of love which is found between friends. Without this sentiment men are liable to become exclusive. Bad and unprofitable friends are shunned but good and profitable friends are trusted. This has always been one of the unchanging factors in human society.

Human society cannot do without the virtue of friendship for a single day. Be that as it may the method of maintaining such friendships is difficult indeed. Unprincipled and deceiving companions seek to gain our confidence and trust. We may be sure, however, that the virtue of friendship is by no means always the plaything of evil-minded men, nor is it hidden always among people of unworthy motives, who do not recognise its beauty. It is but natural that those who observe the teaching of friendship and respect the virtue of mutual trust should prosper. Let us remember also that as in most human affairs if the beginning is not well-conceived the end will be disaster. It is unfortunately true that the same danger lurks in the relations of friendship. The correction of such faults in our national life cannot be neglected for a single day. How can those who have received their being within the pale of this nation, who have been nourished by the august grace of the same Paternal Care, the circumstances of whose lives are identical, who possess the same ancestors, who are united in the same blood relation and trained in the same proprieties, how can such individuals neglect the fundamental relation of friendship? It is indeed natural that among the people of Yamato this teaching should be honoured and the virtue of mutual trust vitally manifested. We are not alone in priding ourselves upon this virtue. We should realise that our prolonged historical existence and the present wealth and prestige which we enjoy are the result of this mutual faith between friends.

It is the true friend who treats us with kindly honesty. It is the true friend who frankly exhorts us to right action. It is the true friend who corrects our faults and points out our evil habits. It is the true friend who leads, advises, and aids us. It is the sympathy of the true friend which completes the task we have failed to accomplish. It is quite true, as foreigners say, that "one's friend is one's second self". If we have a true friend we can indeed say that he is an extension of our own personality. If the relation of true mutual understanding between friends is once established then the purse is common and neither death, nor years, nor disaster can separate. With the deepening of mutual trust even self-sacrifice for the sake of a friend may be gladly endured. What a praiseworthy characteristic of human nature this is! Nevertheless, should we err in the choice of friends, should the method of that choice be mistaken, should our friendship be too hasty and our trust too careless we may enter into friendships that have no permanence. We may find that we have entered into relations that cannot stand the test of danger, and with men who disgrace the name of friendship. As Confucius taught,

Three friends are profitable and three unprofitable. It is profitable to make friends with men who are true, with men who are intelligent, and with men who are cultured. It is unprofitable to make friends of men who have bad habits, who are unprincipled, or who indulge in flattery.

There is much truth in this saying which we should do well to study. By exercising strict care in the selection of our friends we may acquire true friendships.

If we meddle with red ink we are stained by the pigment, if we associate with what is black we are liable to be smudged. This is according to human nature. While it is possible to influence people for good it is equally possible to lead men into such evil habits as will spoil their whole lives. The selection of good friends or evil may have the greatest effect upon the development of our character and talents. How often a true friend has saved a bad man! On the other hand do we not often see evil companions leading the young astray. The harm accruing from an evil friendship may become as destructive as an incurable disease. The poisonous influence of an evil companion may at first be as offensive as a malodorous fishmarket, but in time one may become so accustomed to it as to be utterly unaware of its miasma. Unconsciously infected and led astray many do not recognise their own condition. What awesome results arise from the establishment of good or bad friendships! What infinite care we must take in the selection of our friends! It is but natural that the ancient sages should have emphasised this point.[1]

The wise men of old have taught that we should not make friends of our inferiors. These are indeed golden teachings. A certain commentator has explained that one should not offer to become the friend of an inferior but that the inferior must not be spurned if he evinces a desire for our friendship. I am inclined to think this the true explanation. Another commentator, however, claims that the saying means that one must

[1] For General Nogi's marginal comments on this passage see Appendix, paragraph 17.

deny all friendship to an inferior no matter how greatly he may happen to desire it. If we should carry this comment to its logical conclusion we should end by isolating every man from his fellows. Men are conscious of their superiority to others. If such contentions were followed out through the ranks of the social order each would consider himself superior to some other until finally only one single superior being would be left at the top, and all possibility of friendship eliminated. So applied these words do not show us how to create friendships. Such an explanation is utterly unreasonable and robs this truly golden saying of all meaning. This is indeed an inconsiderate rendering of the ancient saying. In my opinion the warning not to make friends of inferiors means that we should not make friends of unworthy persons. Those who profit us by their companionship should become our good friends. Those who would not become profitable friends we should repudiate, denying intercourse to them. I think that the true meaning of this saying is that we should not have relations with evil and unprofitable friends nor should we repose faith in them. True friends assist each other concealing nothing. Indeed, if we would understand the character of a man, we are told to regard his image in his friend. This is an acceptable saying. The relation of a true friend is infinitely close. If it is necessary for men to have friends then how important it is to select them with care. As it is natural to desire to secure the faith and trust of others all men seek to gain good and profitable friends. Ordinarily we see men selecting profitable friends from among those who evince similarity of taste, of learning, of virtue, of character, courage, talents, physical vigour, wealth, and so forth. What a reasonable method of selecting friends this is! In selecting friends we should pay especial attention to these points.

Once having made a man our friend then no matter what misfortunes he may encounter we must never repudiate the relation. Again, when the above-mentioned conditions are not present it may still be necessary to make friends. Among classmates or those living in the same dormitory even if the friend is not directly profitable we must seek to lead, improve, and develop and in short to fulfil all our duties within the student body. By such mutual support we must seek to secure the best possible conditions within the group. For scholars the highest type of friendship is revealed in the effort to fulfil their obligations by mutual warning, encouragement and the effort to preserve the reputation of the group. Again, even in international relationships as among individuals there are nations which should be admitted to our friendship. Nations with whom we exchange friendship and with whom we establish intimate relations are called friendly nations. Such relations are of the utmost importance in carrying on international affairs. Should they be lacking throughout the world then every nation would for ever have to carry the spear at the ready nor could they at any moment afford to let their hands stray from the sword hilt. With open maps they would ever plan mutual conquests. The earth would be filled with turmoil and peace would be an impossibility. As among individuals so among nations the ones that honour friendship prosper. That nation which observes the full way of righteousness increases in strength. Nations can never afford to neglect the obligations of mutual trust and faith.[1]

I always maintain that mutual trust is the most precious treasure in the world. Without it human society could not exist nor any nation rest in peace for a single day. Without it mankind could not exist in safety. Those who secure such faith in abundance are bound to succeed while those who are unsuccessful here must fail. Upon the amount or degree of such faith achieved depends healthy progress or decadent reaction in human society, the rise and fall of nations, and the prosperity or downfall of families and of individuals. Those who have not the capacity for faith are generally suspicious of others and uneasy of conscience themselves. Lacking the capacity for trust they have no self-confidence. As the rottenness of dead fish is displayed by the presence of maggots and the decay of the tree by the pecking

[1] For General Nogi's marginal comments on this passage see Appendix, paragraph 18.

of birds so are those who are lacking in the social virtues betrayed by their inability either to inspire trust or to believe in others. This is only natural. If men mutually suspect and repudiate each other it inevitably follows that nations will become mutually aggressive and individuals incline to mutual destruction. Should human affairs ever reach such a pass it will be as difficult to direct the destinies of a nation as it is to control six horses with a rotten rope. Is it not true that in ancient times Prince Kwan observed his covenant with Somatsu? Is it not true that Prince Bun of Shin did not take advantage of Sen? Is it not true that Prince Bun of Gi did not break his promise to the people of Gu? Nevertheless in those days it was the common practice of states to put their trust in deception and by the employment of tricks and unprincipled policies to endeavour to conquer the domains of others and destroy their people. As a consequence an age of great decadence lacking in all mutual faith supervened. Was it not at this time that these three princes refused to sacrifice faith to selfish gain? Mutual trust is indeed a perfect policy and the origin of true merit, profit, and glory. How precious is this trust! Friendship is truly founded on mutual faith. For this reason mutual trust between friends has from ancient times been regarded as one of the five cardinal virtues. The glory of our Emperor is as dazzling as the noonday sun and our unique and single Dynasty is for ever immutable and unchangeable. Our people devote themselves loyally to the pursuit of righteousness nor have they at any time permitted the aggression of the foreigner. Family by family they have prospered and each man has lifted up his voice of praise for the blessings of the Sacred Reign. Throughout our history our people have ever firmly, continuously, and perfectly observed the virtue of mutual trust and faith. To say that the faithful observance of high and low alike has implemented the realisation of our great national Destiny is no exaggeration. The unswerving adherence of the people of Yamato to the virtue of mutual trust is one of our chief glories and one which the whole world unites in regarding with respectful admiration. What a marvel is this!

CHAPTER XVII

Modesty and Frugality

THE powerful weapons of a nation's might are not gilded helmets nor iron armour. They are the virtues of the people. The trenchant arms of national power are neither mighty vessels nor powerful guns. The nurture of the national character is the basis of its prestige. As good subjects of Japan we are under obligation to control our lives with care, to cultivate our characters, and to display virtuous manners. In olden days this people was ever deeply conscious of its obligations and responsibilities, but in this present time we seem to be drifting away from these ideals of self-control and the cultivation of character. Although the teaching of ethics and morals is widespread indeed, the actual achievement of these ideals is rare. I regard the neglect of the teachings of Nippon Shindo to be detrimental to the nation as a whole. Therefore, I cannot permit the least defect in the theory and practice of this teaching. I cannot rest satisfied with anything less than the complete apprehension and observance of these sanctions. I cannot allow the slightest alteration. It is a foregone conclusion that the prosperity or the decline of the Empire follows as a consequence on the enforcement or relaxation of Nippon Shindo. My reason for urging the observance of Nippon Shindo is not solely for the purpose of exalting loyalty and filial piety. This teaching is also most valuable in connection with many other aspects of Japanese morals. Modesty and frugality are not merely beautiful characteristics and virtues of the Japanese people. They are the very supports and pillars of the Empire. We should secrete these virtues in the innermost recesses of our hearts and never neglect the obligations they impose upon us for a single day.

From of old the outstanding characteristics of the people of Yamato have been gentleness towards others and forbearance among themselves. Although as a people they are not quarrelsome, preferring to maintain peaceful relations with all men, yet are they never content to play a cowardly rôle. Nor are they willing to waste their lives in empty idleness. They exert themselves diligently to fulfil all their duties and obligations and to observe the claims of Shindo. None will deny that the correct attitude towards others is one of respect or that our own personal habits should be governed by a becoming modesty. Nevertheless, we must avoid carrying either of these virtues to unreasonable extremes. If we do we are in danger of being despised as mere flatterers, or as weak characters. Although respect is undoubtedly a means of maintaining our reputation unimpaired we must also remember that this very virtue of modesty may easily become a source of shame to us or the basis of repudiation on the part of others. It is essential for us to recall that there is but a hair's breadth of difference between the respect due to true modesty and the contempt aroused by effeminacy. Modesty has an inner and an outer aspect. The virtue of modesty consists in maintaining an inner attitude of peaceful calm and an outward aspect of correct formality. On the one hand we are to avoid the least suspicion of pride and on the other we are to conduct ourselves so as not to merit the contempt of others. Each and every subject of the Emperor unites in lauding this virtue of modesty. Each performs his duties within his appointed sphere and never seeks to rise above his proper station in life. At the same time each individual refrains from harming every other individual. The praise of our Imperial land increases with the practice of this virtue. Firmly enshrined in our innermost hearts is the determination to maintain the virtue of modesty in all its beauty, permitting neither failure nor defect in its realisation.

It is incumbent upon the wise not to waste their possessions in luxurious living. It is their duty to avoid all extravagance while carefully building up their fortunes and making preparation for famine, disaster, the violence of nature and the attacks of destructive humanity. Those who desire to establish their families upon a firm foundation, those who wish their nation to be powerful and wealthy must adopt such precautions.

Who is there that does not acknowledge the necessity of making preparation to-day for the morrow? Those who realise that the present is but the premise of the future govern themselves with frugality. With the balance made available by such living they prepare for the future misfortune. Thus they repair the skylights before heaven sends the downpour. The dazzling splendour of our national achievement grows ever brighter and the renown of the Japanese people ever more brilliant because they cultivate true frugality, and avoiding luxury, refuse to waste their substance in selfish pleasures. These virtues which are the basis of true progress advance the propitious destiny of our Empire. Their cultivation has ever been one of the most precious aspirations of the citizens of Japan. Although the nation is at present self-contained and every home sufficient to itself we must not forget that international competition is growing daily more ruthless, or that the pressure of social conditions is constantly becoming more severe. At such a time as this, therefore, we should not forget that our property and possessions must on the one hand be employed to maintain the present degree of prosperity, while on the other a portion should be laid aside for the future. The Japanese subject is under the pressing obligation of living a simple and frugal life. Even in the least details of food and clothing luxury should not be permitted and care should be taken to curtail expenditure. The practice of such frugality, however, is not merely with a view to the future. The observance of the claims of frugality is one of the characteristic virtues of the Japanese people. It is self-evident that the prosperity of the nation at large and of each individual in it must inevitably increase in proportion as this virtue is cultivated.

Kaibara Ekiken in his "Kunshikun"[1] has written,

The ancient sages teach that in the government of a country and a people three things are essential. These three things are good

---

[1] Kaibara Ekiken (1630–1714) was the greatest social teacher of the Tokugawa Age and by many regarded as the foremost exponent of Shushi Confucianism. The title of the notable work here referred to may be rendered in English "A Gentleman's Guide to Correct Morals and Etiquette".

administration, suitable education, and righteous punishments. The
"samurai" is granted his sustenance by his lord and encouraged to
cultivate the virtues, while avoiding gainful pursuits. For the
agricultural worker the burden of public works is made as light as
possible. The tax upon his product is reduced and he is encouraged
to direct his chief energies to the tilling of the soil, the cultivation
of the mulberry and the flax, and the weaving of cotton cloth. The
artisan is encouraged and his products praised, while at the same time
he is forbidden to fashion useless articles of luxury. The commerce
of the merchant is facilitated and the burden of his taxation controlled.
The price of commodities is fixed and he is forbidden to make unreasonable profit by the sale of curious and useless articles. Furthermore good government will prohibit all idleness and forbid all
luxurious living, at the same time encouraging frugality and maintaining all the subjects in a state of contentment with their lot and
their sphere, at all times exhorting them to apply themselves diligently
to their respective duties, that they may have sufficient and never
fall into want. This is the way to govern a people well. Those who
would govern benevolently must first of all practise the virtue of
frugality. Frugality means the avoidance of luxury. It means the
avoidance of wasteful extravagance in clothing or in residence, and
in fact in all matters pertaining to the home. Although a country
may be great in extent the amount of its agricultural products and
its other forms of wealth is limited. If this treasure is wasted by the
extravagant whims of irresponsible rulers then year by year the margin
of insufficiency will increase. Again annual harvests vary in volume.
If rulers persist in a wasteful expenditure of substance then eventually
it will become impossible to observe public formalities properly,
preparation for emergencies will be neglected, and it will be impossible to render assistance to the poor. Finally, in such a state,
the lower class will be oppressed and by reason of debt the state will
not be able to honour its commitments. It will sink into that perilous
condition, in which all benevolent government becomes an impossibility. Wise rulers have always honoured the claims of frugality.
Frugality truly adorns a ruler. Long ago in the reign of Emperor Gyō
there was a great flood which lasted for nine years. During the reign
of King Tō of In there was a drought of seven years. Nevertheless

the subjects of those monarchs did not suffer because frugality had been practised and high and low alike had prepared for evil days. Later, however, an extravagant style of living became the fashion, expenditure increased year by year, and even under ordinary conditions the income was found insufficient. When a poor harvest came high and low suffered alike. This was due to the fact that frugality had been neglected, and no thought taken of the future.

I should like to say here that the house that accumulates deeds of charity will enjoy future prosperity and that the house which practises frugality will enjoy abundance. In books of morals we are taught that the man who practises frugality in his personal habits is virtuous, but that the man who insists upon frugality in his dealings with others is miserly. If we carry frugality too far it may become avarice. Avaricious people are ostracised and despised by worthy persons. Subjects of Japan should observe the obligations of frugality without falling into the error of avarice. Nevertheless, as there is but a hair's breadth of distinction between frugality and avarice we should do well to cultivate this virtue with extreme care in order that we may avoid the error of avaricious habits.

Modesty and frugality are virtues which our Emperor ever desires to see practised. His subjects cultivate these virtues at all times regretting only that they can but imperfectly realise them. Respect and frugality are virtues in which it is easy to experience failure. As Yūshi[1] has written, "If a promise be approximate to the right it will be for ever. If respect be governed by propriety one may escape shame. If reliance is placed upon proper persons it is a good precedent".[2] Although it is true that the observance of frugality is liable to degenerate into the abuse of avarice, and the practice of modesty decay into a mere

[1] A prominent disciple of Confucius.
[2] A good example of the classic tradition at its cryptic best. It is almost impossible to render the quotation into ordinary English. For the benefit of students of Japanese the romanised transliteration is given:
"Shingi ni chikakereba gen fumubeki nari, kyōrei ni chikakereba chijoku ni tōzakaru nari, yoru koto sono shin wo ushinawazareba, mata sō to subeki nari".

effeminacy, yet we who are subjects of Japan can never afford to neglect the careful cultivation of these virtues. In replying to the query of Shikin Shiko[1] stated that Confucius was called in to discuss matters of government because he was possessed of the five virtues of gentleness, goodness, respect, frugality, and humility. According to the proverb, "Pride results in loss but humility is profitable". The respectful man is humble and does not despise others. The frugal man is temperate in his heart and does not covet the possessions of others. Mencius has taught that, "The modest man repudiates no one while the frugal man never covets the possessions of others. Proud and covetous rulers fear only that their subjects may be lacking in servility to them. How can such rulers be truly modest and frugal?" The virtues of modesty and frugality cannot be achieved by mere words or outward appearances. What painstaking cultivation these virtues demand! When we recall that the Japanese people have a tradition with respect to these virtues which is like a glorious heirloom from their past, when we recall that the august rule of our Emperor abounds in all virtues, it is not strange that we should continue to accumulate the treasures of these virtues of modesty and frugality. We should not forget, however, that there can never be an overcultivation of these virtues. In the words of Junshi "Excessive pride is the source of misfortune among men. Modesty and frugality are weapons which will hold at bay powerful encircling foes. The virtues of modesty and frugality are more to be trusted than the points of many spears". This saying is surely not without truth. How deeply should we who are citizens of Japan carve these virtues upon our hearts!

[1] Another prominent disciple of Confucius.

CHAPTER XVIII

Benevolence

TO glory in their pride and to set up barriers of superiority to others, to be prejudiced against other people and suspicious of them, these are not characteristics of the people of Yamato. Possessed by nature of broad sympathies and benevolent dispositions they practise humility, and avoiding senseless pride, succour the weak, fearless of the powerful. This is the true nature of the people of Yamato, this is the flesh and bone of their character handed down from the ancestors. These are among the special virtues which distinguish them. With innate self-denial and true courtesy, observing well the virtues of charity and philanthropy, they repudiate neither foreigner nor barbarian, they cherish the orphan and succour the friendless, they are kind to strangers and friendly to neighbours, they welcome arrivals and speed the parting guest. With these characteristics the nature of the people of Yamato overflows. Abroad these virtues result in the formation of fast friendships with other nations. At home they redound to the renown of the Empire and enrich the ever-growing splendour of the Emblem of the Rising Sun, which floats for ever over this lonely Island Empire of eastern Asia.

In time of peace we must never neglect the possibility of war. Both civil and military affairs must receive our close attention. In time of peace the chiefs of civil departments and the military staff as well must be nurtured and developed. Both organisations must be perfected. When absolutely unavoidable we must bring our weapons resolutely into play in defence of our country, yet we must always remember that it is our responsibility to be benevolent, to act righteously, and to observe fully the claims of humanity, unswayed by prejudice. These heaven-born qualities and characteristics of the people of Yamato it is our duty to cultivate and display. The cultivation of such virtues will ensure our lasting happiness and prosperity.

Although the roof of the Imperial dwelling might leak an

Emperor refused to rethatch. Though the plaster was falling he refused to have it repaired. Observing, however, the clouds of smoke arising from the kitchen fires of his subjects he declared, "I am rich", and his countenance was suffused with joy. On a cold night he cast aside the covers of his bed that he might express sympathy for the sufferings of the poor.[1] He was concerned even with the boots worn by the soldiery.[2] If such be the heart of our august Emperor how greatly must all his subjects rejoice! The whole world proffers heart-felt reverence to the benevolent virtues of the present Emperor. That foreign nations should envy the wonderful privileges of our people, the happy subjects of this glorious Empire, is indeed not hard to understand. The peoples of the east and the west are edified and uplifted by the lofty virtues and the august benevolence of our Emperor and tender him their deep reverence and respectful regard. By such virtues is his rule enhanced and his warlike vigour displayed, while all the world is refreshed by the dews of his grace. Even among the distant peoples of the two hemispheres we are a perpetual envy on account of the superior virtues of our Emperor. Black and white alike throng to our shores not merely on account of our progress in civilisation and culture but because they would reside under the gracious protection and paternal grace of our Imperial Ruler.

There are individuals who through differences in nature and environment hold widely disparate opinions. They seek to achieve the object of their ambitions by various methods. There are some who make passionate appeals to reform professing thereby that they would secure a greater national solidarity. There are others who like fierce birds of prey dare to attempt the subjection of the whole earth. There are those who take a reactionary stand and desire to dig deeper moats and erect loftier walls between themselves and surrounding countries. There are others who recommend an aggressive policy and the

[1] Up to this point the reference seems to be to the well-known story of the Emperor Nintoku (313–400) noted for his benevolence and charity.

[2] This sentence seems to refer unmistakably to the Emperor Meiji. Attention is thus drawn to significant points of similarity in the characters of the two great Emperors.

preparation of military forces in order to produce a multitude of heroes and reinstate a feudal system. Such tendencies are bound to overthrow national solidarity. They are a source of anxiety to wise leaders. Yet in how many lands these unfortunate tendencies are visible to-day! These things are historical facts which need no argument. Our Empire, however, has never fallen into such pitfalls but stands aloof in lonely isolation like Mount Fuji, upon the eastern shores. This happy state is alone due to the lofty virtues of our Emperor ceaselessly manifest in the paternal care of his myriad subjects.

Human nature is full of pride and self-love. It is but natural that black races should make much of their points of superiority and that the white races should pride themselves upon their great qualities. Neither yellow nor white is content to remain behind his fellow. If one race achieves progress the other desires to emulate it. In this fierce struggle the weak are subjugated and the small destroyed. After all the purpose of this struggle seems to be a desire to gain the respect of others and to fill one's own mouth and belly. Sometimes it takes the form of an attempted adjustment of the international balance of power. Again the same tendency finds expression in the calling of a peace conference. These things appear reasonable on the surface but a too facile trust should never be reposed in them. There are times, however, when we must give such proposals our diplomatic assent. Indeed, no matter how many different phases human history may pass through, this underlying international situation must remain the same. Wise men of all ages have deplored and disliked this state of affairs. Here, however, our Empire stands aloft above the rest of mankind, the grateful recipient of an august Imperial Line inviolate for a thousand epochs. From of old its power and prosperity have steadily increased and its noble destiny unfolded before the eyes of men. It is beautiful with the superior beauty of Lake Biwa filled to the brim with crystal waters. Such dazzling achievement is not without adequate basis. It is due to the unchanging devotion of the myriad subjects of this land who have ever devoted themselves to the fulfilment of their whole duty to the Imperial Ruler.

To suppress evil when it arises, to practise righteousness, to discriminate well between that which is good and that which is evil, to enforce the class obligations, to comfort the old and the young, the lonely and the helpless, to reprimand the violent and the avaricious, these are among the special virtues of the people of Yamato. From prehistoric times to the present day they have never turned aside from this path. In the spirit of these virtues they welcome the stranger and speed the parting guest and treat with fraternal love peoples of widely different race and colour, while at home they never set up the slightest barriers between themselves and foreign peoples. These fundamental qualities of the people of Yamato are alone due to the paternal solicitude of our Sacred Emperor. Indeed his benevolent grace is not confined to humanity alone but extends to all living creatures, to the bird and the insect, to fish and shell fish, alike to grass and tree. Without distinction he devotes his nourishing care to their well-being and all things feel the influence of his paternal solicitude, as the grasses of the field bend in unison beneath the summer breeze. How great are the lofty virtues of our Emperor! By this influence evil tendencies are restrained and virtues cultivated among the people of Yamato. The gentle kindliness and the trustworthy faithfulness of the people of Yamato which never change or fail toward all objects and all duties are indeed due to this single and unique source.

No matter what changes may take place elsewhere upon this earth, while our Emperor enjoys prosperity, the gracious winds and abundant rains shall not fail upon the land. His power and virtuous prestige acknowledged and revered throughout the world grow ever more glorious and clear, rivalling the brilliant beams of the sun and the moon. Under his guidance we cultivate friendly relations with all mankind while developing the true virtues at home. It is thus that we are enabled to support and uphold the Throne. We laud his sacred wisdom, bespeak for him length of days in our prayers, and earnestly desire the lasting peace and prosperity of Yamato.

CHAPTER XIX

The Cultivation of Learning

WHO would be satisfied with primitive conditions or for ever content with a barbarous state of society? As soon as men have energy to spare above the necessities of bare existence they cultivate literature and morals. In the present age the number of those who devote themselves to learning and the search for truth increases daily. From the university at the top to the primary school at the bottom the various phases of the educational system have been carefully arranged. From the studies which require special research to the most ordinary sciences everything has been provided for. Civilisation and culture are daily advanced and their refinements grow ever more common until the atmosphere of culture extends throughout the whole land. How glorious is this spectacle! In this day, when like a myriad raging torrents mingling their tumultuous waters the civilisations of the world contend for mastery and in the midst of fierce competition develop their knowledge, enhance their refinement and gain fame and renown, in this day wherein all nations compete upon the stage of living human affairs in a vigorous display of their abilities, we cannot endure to fall behind or to be superseded. No sacrifice or hardship is too great if we are thereby enabled to achieve our objective and ride our steed triumphantly to the summit of Mount Go.[1] We who have such an ideal before us must strive to realise it, never permitting relaxation in the quest or allowing ourselves to fall into the luxury of idle habits. Coursing ever forward upon the tide of world progress, in the rank of the five great powers, the glorious destiny of our Empire displays to-day a more brilliant success than in any previous epoch of our history. To-day we take our place triumphantly and successfully in the midst of

[1] A reference to an incident in Chinese history. In the war between Go and Etsu the warriors of Etsu were completely victorious and were thus able to ride their chargers to the topmost peaks of Go, hence the proverbial expression.

those fierce contentions of international competition. How great must be the effort of those upon whom rests the responsibility of achieving and realising our national progress.

Scientific studies in our land have reached the region of recondite research and the subdivisions of the most advanced enquiry have greatly multiplied. A multitude of books has been produced and research becomes ever more minute. Throughout the land voices raised in learning may be heard on every hand. No locality lacks its school. No matter where we may go there is not a single village boy ignorant of his letters. In no town within the land can we find even an illiterate labourer. The cultivation of learning is regarded with increasing respect. Learning has prospered and research has become exceedingly minute.

The student who would excel must first pass through the lower schools before he can enter the course for specialists. In ancient times three courses were open to the student. Those who were not attracted by Buddhist learning became Shintoists. The remainder adopted Confucianism. Although the object of their belief differed unity of aspiration led them all to apply themselves to learning and the cultivation of their characters. In this respect I believe we may say that their purpose was identical. Since the Restoration, however, a great variety of cultural currents has been diverted into our country. The tide of these recent tendencies has had a violent effect upon both Government and people. It has undoubtedly led to great advances in the civilisation of the Empire. At the same time great changes have been instituted in the methods and means of acquiring an education. People differ in their allegiance to the cultural leadership of England, France, Germany, or America. Despite the many tendencies, however, the great object of cultivating this foreign learning is the production of an individual adapted to the times and the training of leaders who will be capable of directing the present generation with a leadership which will be of permanent value. It matters not whether we adopt the culture of England, of France, of Germany, or of

America. Our only purpose is to select the superior elements in each, supply thereby our own deficiencies and eliminate what may be of inferior value. Although our country is small and our people few in number it is our purpose by such efforts to render powerful and great this Empire, situated upon the eastern confines of the Asiatic continent, securing for her that progress and development which will enable her to take her rightful place upon the stage of world-wide human affairs.

As learning advances men realise that the area of the unknown grows ever greater. At the same time specialisation becomes progressively more intricate until it seems as though there would be no end to the multiplication of different departments of research. As learning advances we are able to penetrate into many deep and intricate problems of which the preceding generation had no conception. Men of learning are constantly being rewarded with praise for having surpassed their masters. In such an age as this, therefore, the acquisition of learning must never be neglected. Those who would sail upon the great ocean of learning must not fear the powerful waves upon its surface. Those who would travel the road of learning must not be dismayed at the intricacies of its windings. If we have the true will to learn, if we are not lacking in manly courage and determination, it will not be impossible for us to achieve such a success that our contemporaries may come to rate us as great scholars.

Humanity prides itself on being the lord of creation. Among men we pride ourselves upon being a superior people. Let us enquire the source of this superiority. In the first instance it is undoubtedly due to that heaven-inspired spirit of progressive aspiration coupled with a cautious conservatism which we possess. But it is also true that our whole-hearted application to learning and our single-hearted devotion to education stimulate these qualities into vigorous life. It is due to the possession of this spirit that we are able to achieve a successful advance in many directions. At the same time it is due to our cautious conservatism that we are able to escape many pitfalls. I believe that this combination of progressive radicalism and cautious conservatism will continue to secure to us the rank of a superior people and that it will permanently establish our renown as a great and civilised nation. If the possession of these qualities informs our appreciation of the international situation, controls our view of internal affairs, motivates a useful introspection, and stimulates in us a true desire for learning then there is nothing in the world that we as a people need fear. No matter how eager our aspirations, no matter how vigorous our determination, if we fail to apply ourselves to learning, if we are lacking in true education, we are no better than barbarians or blind men who have lost their staves. If we refuse to listen to the teachings of others and push on without knowledge of the course we shall be fortunate indeed if our uncultivated energy does not finally lead us into the futile peril of a man who rushes to attack a tiger empty-handed, or one who would attempt to ford a great river on foot. We do not aspire to the exhibition of such senseless energy. Our energy needs to be great and vigorous indeed, yet we must learn to realise the absolute necessity of controlling and directing this energy by the mastery of learning and all the arts. If to the mastery of learning there is added a courageous valour the combination is bound to produce great men and cultured leaders in human society. As subjects of this Empire we must all determine to pursue such an objective.

In order to achieve a fitting culture and thereby repay our debt to our country we should carefully cultivate self-respect, self-reliance, and self-knowledge, in addition to the performance of our other duties. In order to succeed in the cultivation of these qualities we must first apply ourselves to the acquisition of an education and the refinement of our personalities. At the same time we should take care to avoid the pitfalls of a merely superficial education. According to the saying, "Propriety, integrity, uprightness, and honour are the four strands which sustain the state. Unless they are firmly stretched the nation will collapse ". How true this is! How obvious it is that nothing will be gained, no matter how great our aspirations and no matter how deep our learning, unless we have first cultivated the virtues! How unfortunate it would be if those who devote themselves to learning should fall into the error of regarding it as the only end of life! How gratefully must the citizens of this Empire acknowledge these truths!

CHAPTER XX

The Mastery of a Profession

I N ancient times when the standards of civilisation were low and requirements simple men were satisfied if they were able to obtain suitable clothing, food, and lodgings. These three requirements were necessities even in the simplest state of society. With the advance of human civilisation the nature and quality of men's requirements developed and greatly increased in number. They were no longer limited to the satisfaction of the three basic necessities. To-day the demand for the satisfaction of an ever-increasing multitude of new requirements on the part of society is becoming clamorous indeed. In order to satisfy the material and mental needs of the present age each individual must do his part in increasing national wealth and national production by the industrious cultivation of his business or profession. If this is an obligation which all the world acknowledges how much more must it be the supreme duty of the subjects of this land, which stands in lofty grandeur upon the borders of eastern Asia!

As human beings in this world it is our true destiny to master some profession or trade and by means of honest labour to seek to acquire the elements of a worthy and sober livelihood. Those who step aside from the true way of life and attempt to succeed dishonestly are hated even by the most ordinary people. Those who in their daily life are lacking in trustworthiness, in diligence, and in endurance in their application to profession or trade, and those who would dissipate their fortunes cannot hope to escape disaster. When vulgar men become reduced in circumstances they prey upon society. Such people eventually pass beyond the hope of salvation. On account of excessive misery they lose all sense of correct principles. People with fixed principles desire to live as law-abiding and peaceful subjects of the Emperor. Failure to realise this ideal is sometimes due to the fact that men attempt to cultivate fixed principles without seeing the necessity or making the effort to obtain first of all some fixed property. Although it may be extreme to declare that those who are without fixed property are lacking in fixed principles it is nevertheless true that the majority of such people lack such principles and have already fallen into a state of drifting dissipation, idle amusements, and even vagabondage. If we desire to possess fixed principles and to follow the true course in life we cannot afford to neglect the acquisition of property. This is the correct procedure.

A nation cannot exist for a single day without a settled policy. Without definite policies or fixed objectives a nation is certainly in as perilous a condition as a small boat tossed hither and thither while floating amid the raging seas. The maintenance of the dignity and integrity of a state depends to a great degree upon a fixed national policy. Furthermore, a good economic foundation is essential if the state is to realise that national policy and take its proper place among the nations of the world. For a country to insist upon its policies or endeavour to demonstrate its power and prestige, while its national treasure is insignificant and its people poor, is like trying to move a train without supplying it with motive power. To attempt such a course is to act like a fool. As the success of a national policy depends upon the accumulation of national treasure it is necessary that the people should be united in purpose and possessed of fixed principles by means of a thorough training in the proper method of amassing wealth. The accumulation of the national treasure depends upon the diligent application of the people. The diligent toil of the subject renders the national life vigorous, active, competent, successful, and brilliant. When the subjects are financially successful they are able to maintain their individuality and rightly observe fixed principles. Therefore, it is incumbent upon all to apply themselves to the mastery of trade or profession. Each must endeavour to amass treasure and develop the means of making money. Thus both as a nation and as individuals this people must press courageously forward to the fulfilment of its destiny. All loyal subjects of the Empire must apply themselves to the mastery of profession or trade and by this means supply the necessary elements required by the Empire for the fulfilment of its mission.

In ancient times the occupations of the people were elementary and a state of competition did not exist. With the advance of human wisdom and the growing complexity of social organisation the selection of an occupation has become of necessity a more difficult thing. At the present time the progress of human culture has the wild impetuosity of the boat propelled downstream in the midst of the swiftest current. In this age of highly developed means of communication the intercourse of countries thousands of miles apart is easier than that of ancient villages which could even hear the faint crow of a cock or the bark of a dog across the intervening distance. In such an age as this all must exercise the greatest care in the selection of an occupation. The choice of a profession depends in the first instance upon the natural ability of each individual. This selection, however, is not entirely limited by the talents of the individual. It is absolutely essential to consider the bearing of this selection upon the general question of the prosperity of the nation. In view of the fact that the selection of a profession depends both upon the talents of the individual and the circumstances in which the nation finds itself it is incumbent upon us to avoid strictly that mischievous and foolish idea which would always limit the son to the profession of his father. Among the many nations which at present stand established in the world there are states both small and great, both weak and powerful. There are states impregnable as mountains and others vulnerable as eggshells. There are some nations whose prosperity is founded upon agriculture and others which find their chief advantage in the development of commerce and industry. Whether they specialise in civil or military arts each fulfils its own destiny and endeavours to lay a sound foundation of national wealth. Again, as the individual is possessed of his own special gifts and has his own individual destiny to fulfil it behoves him to apply himself wisely to his profession, keeping these governing circumstances always in mind. In a general sense each individual must consider the true source of national prosperity, and in an individual sense each one must, with the utmost care, conserve his property from loss. What is the best means of caring for one's property? The only way is by applying one's self with industry to the cultivation of a profession. We must remember also that trades and professions change in nature and aspect with the daily advance of civilisation. Again, some men go abroad and seek their fortunes in foreign lands. Some may go abroad as colonists and emigrants and seek to amass wealth during a temporary residence in foreign countries. There are others again who remain at home and seek to enhance the wealth and prestige of family and nation by more direct methods. At the present time there are in this country innumerable trades and professions which arise out of the complexities of modern civilisation, and are connected with manufactories, commercial enterprises, banks, railways, mines, and many other forms of industry and commerce. Therefore, it is necessary to determine carefully the proper proportion of national effort which is to be allotted to civil and military occupations, taking into consideration the present and probable future circumstances of our nation. We must realise that we are always confronted with these exceedingly important problems.

Long ago a certain distinguished teacher gathered his pupils about him in the university and taught them that "Skill is enhanced by application and lost in idleness. Morality is achieved through careful practice and lost through lack of effort". These golden words are not merely precious precepts fit for the ears of learned men. They are of vital consequence to all ranks of society and to all men engaged in the pursuit of their trades and professions. If we devote ourselves with diligent application to the mastery of our business and the cultivation of our profession then we may have no fear that we shall not be able to master the most intricate details of trade secrets or the mysteries of science. Furthermore, as we become proficient in these details our study and absorption will increase in proportion. With the increase of interest and absorption will come the final mastery of the details. Indeed the thorough mastery of a trade or profession, a whole-hearted concentration upon it, and a true devotion to his heaven-granted mission constitute the ultimate and highest duty of every loyal citizen.

CHAPTER XXI

The Development of the Intellect

TO achieve a higher development and to attain true progress in learning and in the cultivation of the intellect are impulses common to the whole of humanity. To endeavour by this means to gain true success and prosperity is indeed a thoroughly natural course. Hence the cultivation of the mental faculties is a matter of vital importance which must never be neglected.

No human being can ever be content to remain in a state of benighted ignorance. All men endeavour to escape from a state of ignorance by careful effort. Throughout the past history of the race this type of aspiration has been continuously manifest, while in this present day it is universal. This is equally true whether we consider the individual, the small community, the great province, the country at large, or even the world as a whole. All alike endeavour to follow the same course. No one will deny the statement that the voice of the reader grows ever louder in the land or that the facilities for education are ever more complete. The steady advance in human culture arises from this very impulse. Not only is the cultivation of intellectual faculties essential to us as human beings, such obligations have even greater weight for us as citizens of the Empire.

From primary school to university well-ordered and systematic courses of study have been arranged. Throughout the whole country educational facilities have been provided for all kinds of study. Neither practical sciences nor theoretical lack suitable facilities for research. In the departments of law and political economy, of the applied sciences, of agriculture, of commerce, of literature, and of religion, bachelors and doctors are being produced in ever-increasing numbers. At the same time substantial scientific progress is being realised in every department of advanced enquiry. As water seeks its own level and as fire consumes dry fuel so the cultivation of mental faculties demands an individual effort in order to achieve results. The methods of acquiring intellectual power through the exertion of one's efforts are so numerous that we cannot pause to describe them in detail. Nevertheless, they can be divided, in general, into those studies which can be pursued at home and those which require residence abroad. There are some who travel in foreign lands in order to enrich their minds. There are others who, while remaining at home, devote themselves to a close study of native and foreign learning. By the mastery of numerous subjects they become deeply learned in the most recondite mysteries and the most intricate details of science. On every hand we observe the growing popularity and advancement of scientific research. As a consequence the daily life of our country is enriched by the practical application of these scientific discoveries. To such factors as these is due our wonderful progress and the present degree of civilisation achieved by our Empire.[1]

In the sphere of learning there is no difference of rank, as between the scholars. There is neither great nor small, rich nor poor, east nor west. All are equally able to reach their goal if they apply themselves diligently to their studies. No matter what reliance we put in rank or in wealth if we fail to apply ourselves to our studies we shall not avoid the stigma of ignorance. By the power of learning alone men are enabled to rise from the lowest orders and to ride their chargers triumphantly to the topmost peaks of "Go". If we cultivate learning diligently without neglecting the least detail, then no matter how lowly our birth we shall succeed in leaving behind us an undying reputation and a scholarly example. When we survey present-day society we find men cultivating the military arts, gaining skill in the craft they have selected, adding to their wisdom, and by a careful cultivation repairing their own deficiencies from the excellences of others. Applying themselves diligently to such activities they fear nothing so much as an insufficient achievement. To stand alone in the midst of this highly com-

---

[1] For General Nogi's marginal comments on this passage see Appendix, paragraph 19.

petitive society and to win success is the endeavour of all. Such ambitions are not the sole possession of the white race, nor yet of the black. Every living race that has succeeded in producing a nation centres its hope and endeavour continuously upon such objectives. It is in such objectives and in such purposes that we realise our unity with the peoples of other nations. By a careful cultivation of our intellectual faculties we shall be deemed worthy to unfurl the Banner of the Rising Sun freely and confidently among the nations of the world, and at the same time we shall maintain our prestige as a great power.

Is it not true that in the present age all barriers between our own nation and the other nations of the world have been thrown down and that the evil custom of regarding foreigners as barbarians has been abandoned? Whatever will supply our deficiencies and our lack is welcomed. In fact these features of foreign civilisation and culture pour in upon us from foreign countries like an overwhelming flood. The wisdom of Europe and the science of America are transplanted upon our shores and repair our deficiencies. The things which are needed for our instruction flow into our land with the impetus of a thousand waters. These words describe the situation to-day. Whatever is of profit in Asia is of benefit to Europe and America as well. Although the distance which separates these continents is great nevertheless the reciprocal exchange of benefits is carried on without the slightest let or hindrance. In human history the flesh of the weak soon becomes the food of the strong while the lands of the powerless soon become the possession of the mighty, irrespective of questions of right. What nation is it that stands for ever with calm dignity upon the shores of Asia, that maintains its nationality inviolate, that pursues undetained the course of greatest advantage, and with superlative power within its right, goes to the aid of others, refusing to take advantage of the weak, observing all the obligations of righteousness, and ever governing her deeds by the loftiest sanctions of humanity?

Our Empire, situated upon the outer fringe of eastern Asia, was of old beyond the pale of world movements. When once we had entered the current of world affairs and taken our place upon the stage of international competition we found our way barred in front by the tiger and our rear threatened by the wolf. There must be some special considerations to explain why, although hard-pressed on every hand, we have never yet become the prey of other nations. We have, on the contrary, successfully maintained our existence in the midst of these perils and have won the respectful regard of foreign powers. Although this is due in the first instance to that vigorous and living spirit which pervades the people of Yamato it is also undoubtedly due to the painstaking efforts of those great statesmen and other notables who have carefully observed the progress achieved by other peoples and who have realised clearly the advantages of such things as modern means of communication, the activities which produce national wealth, and in general, all factors which contribute to the enlargement of the power and prestige of a nation. Abroad these men have observed with care the various tendencies of modern civilisation while at home they have devoted themselves to the improvement of the various departments of individual and public life. Leading the people skilfully onward they have carefully adapted them to the requirements of modern society. At all times the subject serves and obeys the Imperial Will, cultivates his individual intellectual gifts, and applies himself to the fulfilment of his obligations in such a manner as to escape the reproach of inferiority. By such diligent application to the cultivation of their intellectual gifts the citizens of this Empire long to repay, even though in slight degree, that August Grace of which they have been the constant recipients. I do not hesitate to state that the subjects of this Empire are ready to sacrifice even life itself in the acquisition of knowledge.

CHAPTER XXII

The Development of Character

IF people possess virtue they are honoured. If they lack it they are distrusted. This respect and this distrust are alike independent of intellectual attainments or physical prowess. The respect or dishonour in which men are held does not by any means depend upon the possession of such qualities. It is the possession of virtue or the lack of it which determines whether we shall respect a man or repudiate him.

Those who possess virtue enjoy inner peace, while its outward display in human contacts never arouses the hostility of mankind. Truly virtuous people are never conscious of anger but are mild-mannered in all their relations. The qualities of the virtuous man influence mankind as the gentle breezes cause the grasses to bend. Virtue never lives solitary among men. Men are attracted to virtue as water seeks its own level. Where virtue is lacking, however, nothing has the power to attract. Men who are lacking in virtue are ostracised by society. It frequently happens that men who have cultivated intellect for its own sake become the mere slaves of reason and often end by occupying themselves with knowledge of a harmful character, which they employ in deceitful undertakings. The cultivation of the intellect and the acquisition of virtue are two separate things.[1] Here are two kinds of effort whose goal is separate and distinct. Intellect and character are not mutually inclusive. He who would be a leader in the sphere of knowledge should at least expend an equal effort in the cultivation of virtue. Even those who already possess the talents calculated to make them leaders must give sufficient attention to the cultivation of virtue if they wish to attain true success, either as individuals or as subjects. It is the duty of learned and ignorant alike to cultivate virtue fearing ever their own insufficiency in this respect.

[1] For General Nogi's marginal comments on this passage see Appendix, paragraph 20.

Lacking wings men have never been able to soar above the clouds, lacking ferocious claws they have never been able to overcome their enemies by means of the physical endowments of nature. How then have they successfully held the sovereignty of creation for a thousand epochs? It is without doubt due to the fact that in human society the weak have not always been the prey of the strong, nor have the strong always oppressed the weak. There has ever shone among men a light which has brightly illuminated human society. It is due also to that elixir of peaceful submission which has always encouraged harmonious relations. The reason for that success with which our Empire has established its reputation and maintained its rank among the other great powers is found on the one hand in the wise rule of our Sacred Emperor and on the other in the willing obedience of all subjects to the August Will, coupled with a careful attention to the cultivation of true virtue. As the saying has it, "Wealth brings prosperity to the house, while virtue enriches the life of the individual". It is indeed true that all men, whether distinctly conscious of it or not, really desire to be led by and to be admitted on terms of intimacy with the truly virtuous man. Friendly relations among men and the survival of the weak in human society must also depend upon the existence and manifestation of virtue. Should virtue once be withdrawn human society would quickly degenerate and become as hopelessly tangled as a ravelled skein. The mutual enmity of men would soon become more terrible than the horrors of the inferno of mutual destruction. Thus considered none can avoid a recognition of the incalculable value of these three things, benevolence, righteousness, and true humanity. Nothing has greater power to enrich and bless mankind than these three virtues. How necessary it is to cultivate virtue! We who are subjects of the Empire must ever consider it our most urgent responsibility.

The obligations of virtue are acknowledged throughout the whole world, while the problem of its realisation unites the history of the past with that of the present. It is most gratifying to note that the number of those who exhort us to live virtuously increases daily. Nevertheless, it is unfortunate that this exhortation is too often limited to words and not realised in conduct. People are easily moved by attractive theories. Despite the fact that we are exhorted to live virtuously there is, nevertheless, an ever-increasing group of people who abandon themselves to evil conduct. There are indeed many who speak but few who act. I feel impelled to utter a solemn warning with regard to this situation. Those who merely exhort us to adopt virtuous conduct without setting the example themselves must end by casting dishonour on virtue itself. All teachers of ethics should keep this point carefully in mind.

A curious theory has recently become audible. This is the teaching that virtue can be divided into public virtue and private virtue.[1] Is it indeed possible that virtue can be so divided? Virtue is an inseparable thing. It has but a single root and cannot be divided into two elements. It is only possible to make such a distinction with regard to the objects of virtuous conduct. It is only with respect to the direction of its manifestation that we can formulate separate definitions for virtue. Thus the public manifestation of virtue might be called public virtue, while virtue exemplified in personal relations might be called private virtue. Although such a distinction may be valid there is necessity for caution. If public virtue should be loudly recommended at this time when the practice of private virtue is far from perfect it may become the sole object of men, to the complete exclusion of private virtue. This danger occasions me much anxiety. I am convinced that it is unnecessary to recommend either public virtue or private virtue as separate things. On the other hand it is our essential duty to cultivate and perfect ourselves in virtue itself. If true virtue is realised there need be no anxiety with respect to defects in public virtue nor any fears as to the degeneration of private virtue. Our great duty is to avoid neglect in the cultivation of that pure virtue which is the true foundation of all worthy conduct. Virtue must be coextensive

---

[1] For General Nogi's marginal comments on this passage see Appendix, paragraph 21.

with life. The great importance of virtuous conduct has been a tradition handed down from our ancestors, which each successive generation seeks to honour. Our ancestors have always taught the necessity of cultivating virtue. Handed down from father to son this tradition has endured to the present day. We all seek to carve this teaching deeply upon the tablets of our hearts. Since the fulfilment of the obligations of virtue is a task which the subjects of this Empire can never afford to neglect, either by day or by night, since it is the fundamental principle upon which our national life is based, we the citizens of this Empire must make the acquisition of virtuous character the central element of every word and deed. Unethical living can never be countenanced by the citizens of this Empire.

CHAPTER XXIII

The Public Good

TO serve the public good in a self-forgetful manner is the natural duty of all who would function as members of human society. To serve the public interest and to advance the public good are essential conditions of all communal life. To forsake private interest, to give up private desires, to set aside considerations of personal gain, to sacrifice all these things to the public good when the occasion arises, and to devote one's self wholly to the public interest, these are the true duties of every citizen of the Empire. This is an important study which demands our most careful attention.

Let us enquire into some of the causes for the advance or decay of society. For the most part this depends upon the profit or loss sustained by the whole people. The sources of national or group success depend in no small degree upon the care which is taken to secure the success of the individual elements which form these compounds. The prosperity of society, the success of the national organisation, and the happiness of the people as a whole, depend upon service of the public interest, devotion to the advancement of the public good, and concentration upon the general profit of all. If the individual elements which compose society have no conception of the necessity for serving the interests of the whole, if they are lacking in public spirit, if they have no idea of the true significance of society, if they are unable to comprehend the meaning of the national organisation, if they are ignorant of the duties of citizens, then it will not require the art of the fortuneteller to prophesy that senescence and decay which will certainly be their fate. It goes without saying that the public officials who administer the affairs of state should formulate with care the future policies of the Empire. It is also necessary, however, that the citizens should devote their attention to these subjects. The future policies of the Empire depend vitally upon the present promotion of national wealth and the happiness of the people. The realisation of this goal of prosperity and well-being among the people depends upon the extent to which each individual fulfils the obligations of public spirit. While acknowledging these ideals of public spirit we must carefully avoid all errors in respect to the objects toward which it is directed.

We who are citizens of the Empire must remember that we are not only citizens of the Empire of Japan but members also of one great human society. While as citizens of the Empire we take part in the public life of that Empire it is also our duty to co-operate in the public life of the common world society of which we form a component element. We must never neglect this dual obligation but always do our best to further the public interest and increase public prosperity. The public interest is a common duty and not to be limited to the interests of the individual. To sacrifice all personal interest to the public good when the occasion arises is certainly the duty of the citizens of this Empire. When the interests of the broader society conflict with the interests of our country, when these two obligations are not in accord, then we must devote ourselves to the interest of our own country and hasten to its aid. When the two interests coincide we should devote our energies equally to furthering both ends, thus enhancing the happiness and the brotherhood of man while ensuring the glorious prosperity of the Empire of Japan.

The Restoration altered all the aspects of our national life. The feudal system which had persisted in our country for three hundred years was overthrown. The spirit of provincialism and local allegiance was done away with and the whole nation united in vigorous insistence upon the central virtue of loyalty. All came to realise the true obligation of sacrificing the individual interest for the good of the nation. The whole people united in the endeavour to perform this essential duty. Nevertheless, as it is difficult to straighten at once something which has long been bent, so it has been found impossible to eradicate immediately all traces of that local allegiance fostered so long by feudalism. We are therefore not without examples of men in public affairs who serve their own ends and who do not seem to acknowledge the obligation of public interest. Happily this type of leader is becoming continually more rare with the passage of time and disappears day by day like the snows of winter which melt under the warm sun of spring. This is a very gratifying fact. At this time, especially, we should endeavour to arouse that public spirit so long in abeyance. By rendering it vigorous we shall faithfully fulfil our duty as subjects of the Empire. Since the Restoration the whole country has become a single unit. All the nations of the earth now "advance along the rails" of the same international relations. In a sense national obligations have become universal obligations. The social obligations of one society have become the obligations of a world society. Considerations such as these have still further enlarged the conception of public spirit among our people. They now consider the interest of the peoples of the whole world, cement friendships with many foreign nations, and avoid the establishment of all barriers. Where the interests of foreign peoples are concerned we must not limit ourselves to selfish considerations of our own advantage. With hearts as pure as the unclouded moonlit sky we should consider all obligations whether of public or private nature, endeavouring at all times to secure for the nation true advantage and profit. I believe that service of this nature is both the pleasant privilege and the honourable obligation of all the citizens of this new Japan.

As citizens of the Empire I have already declared that we have a dual duty to perform in respect to the question of the service of the public interest. It is true, however, that the opportunities of public service are so numerous that it is difficult to name them all. All examples of what is profitable to the public are forms of the public good. Under certain circumstances private good may become public good. Although it is easy enough to theorise regarding the separation of private and public interest, it is nevertheless a mistake to hold that private interest is always private interest and that it can never be public interest. It is incorrect to hold that public interest and private interest are always mutually exclusive. There are circumstances under which they can be shown to unite. Nevertheless, when private interest and public interest are found to be in conflict we are under obligation to abandon private advantage and to serve public good. Since opportunities for public service increase with the advance of civilisation it is essential that we devote an ever closer degree of care to the question of the public good.

Coincident with the marvellous economic expansion and progress utilitarian ideas have become implanted in the mind of the people. The popularity of such utilitarian concepts has been so great that their influence is noted on every hand, and the number of those who devote themselves wholly to the accumulation of wealth is increasing. Rapid material progress has aroused a spirit of cupidity in the people. Those who would pursue personal profit and advantage lie in wait on every hand like hungry tigers in ambush. In the end people of this description become completely mastered by the idea of self-interest. They devote themselves to the pursuit of self-interest to the exclusion of all considerations of the public good. Unfortunately, we are not without examples of wretched beings of this type who acknowledge no considerations of public good whatever. Although we may sympathise with such persons on the ground that they have been led astray by the recent violent and extensive alterations in society it is nevertheless our duty to utter this solemn warning.

It is necessary to devote one's self both to private and public interest. Nevertheless, we who are citizens of this Empire must be ever ready to sacrifice the private to the public interest, when the occasion demands it. Setting aside considerations of our own interest we devote our lives to the service of the state, fearing nothing so much as some dereliction in respect to this duty. Such is, indeed, the duty of all those who are subjects of the Empire.

CHAPTER XXIV

Occupation

ALL the phenomena of society undergo alteration. On the one hand are seen evolution and progress and on the other degeneration and decay. Although the course and tendency may differ the element of change is constant. With this constant change and the multiplication of activities which we see on every hand society enjoys prosperity and the people accumulate wealth. Therefore, we must always give strict attention to the extension and development of our affairs. How countless are the occupations to which we may devote ourselves! There is no limit to the material or intellectual activities through which we can contribute to the prosperity of the nation. On the one hand we devote ourselves to a careful preservation of the arts of the past while on the other we welcome new activities. While improving the methods of the past we profit also by the study of new inventions. Thus our civilisation grows daily more refined, the social organisation is perfected, and the interests of the nation advanced. Such tasks constitute our true duty and are, at the same time, the sacred will of our Emperor.

That lofty tree which pierces heaven itself originates in the tender shoot. That lofty mountain whose sublime summit challenges the arching sky is yet composed of handfuls of earth. Material phenomena and human affairs are alike in so far as they both proceed toward refinement from coarse and inconsiderable beginnings. All things advance from the simple to the complex. In the course of such development there may be encountered elements which give rise to failure and again other factors which ensure successful progress. Terrestrial change is infinite, boundless, and unfathomable. The conditions of survival in the nomadic prehistoric age when men fished in the waters and hunted upon the mountains differed from the conditions imposed in a later age when human society reached the agricultural stage. Nor again were the conditions of a purely agricultural society suited to be the conditions of survival in a commercial and industrial age. To-day we are completely severed from these prehistoric conditions and are in the act of passing from an agricultural to a commercial and industrial state of society. In such an age how foolish it is to cling obstinately to the past or to proffer unreasoned reverence to what is old. In view of the fact that the conditions of survival alter inevitably with the passage of time we should in the present age consider with care the problem of adaptation and endeavour to win success on the greatest number of counts. This is the true duty of all citizens of the Empire.

The increase of population demands an increase of wealth. In order to increase the wealth of the nation it is necessary to carry on a ceaseless conflict with the forces of nature, to avail ourselves of new resources, and to improve methods of production by a careful mastery of natural laws. The growing refinement of civilisation leads to a great stimulation of mutual intercourse. While this intercourse supplies mutual needs it inevitably gives rise to competition in commerce and industry. In turn this very competition leads to increasing refinements and to the general enrichment of life. To-day all the nations of the earth are assembled on a single "go" board.[1] The whole world is nothing but a mighty stage upon which we may exhibit our abilities. In order to bring about the development of resources and to ensure true progress in human affairs it is essential that each one should apply himself to the mastery of his own occupation and to the complete fulfilment of his obligations. Diligent application to the consummation of our duties is the chief obligation of each and all. We should ever remember that this is the true way of fulfilling the sacred will of our Emperor.

With the growing complexity of modern society the majority of the occupations of mankind cease to be simple. In order to live successfully to-day we must devote ourselves to an infinite variety of vocations. Some must apply themselves to intellectual pursuits while others must devote their whole lives to practical occupations. Though the activities of rural and metropolitan

[1] A game similar to draughts or checkers though more complicated.

populations, of the fisherman on the shore and the woodcutter upon the mountain may differ widely in themselves, nevertheless, all unite in loyal application to their callings and in devotion to the common prosperity. Although the peculiar duties of the warrior, the farmer, the artisan, and the merchant may differ, although some may occupy themselves with the pursuit of learning and others with the cultivation of military arts, although some may devote themselves exclusively to the study of science and others again to the practical affairs of business life, there is not one that neglects to carry out his duties as a human unit. Thus we citizens of the Empire ever apply ourselves with especial diligence to the fulfilment of all our obligations, while putting forth every effort to take advantage of the most recent factors of progress.

How great indeed is the increase of occupations which accompanies the development of civilisation! There is not one form of study whether of the celestial bodies which revolve in the heavens above or of the elements which compose the earth, whether of the mountains or the rivers or the grasses and the vegetation which clothes the fields, that is unconnected with some particular form of occupation. There is no phenomenon in the wide universe which may not become the object of our attention. There is no part of the world which may not become the scene of our activities. It is not surprising that the tide of advancing civilisation should daily bring to our shores an ever-changing procession of occupations. We who stand in the midst of these currents of progress cannot afford to be idle for a single day.

In this day of great steamers upon all the oceans, and of submarine cables, international intercourse has become facile, and commerce and industry have been greatly stimulated both at home and abroad. Foreign as well as native culture is encouraged on every hand. There also seems to be a tendency to seek a certain standardisation of human culture throughout the world. Upon the land are found the railway, the telegraph, the telephone, and many other applications of electricity and steam. Furthermore, progress in the arts of printing, of navigation, and the various facilities for postal communication all favour the rapid advance of civilisation. They in turn stimulate the world of affairs. There follows a constantly accelerated development and advance in all our occupations. Scientific inventions and discoveries affect conditions the world over. When we are considering the positions we are to occupy we can never afford to lose sight of these broader aspects of modern life.

In recent years great advances have occurred in every department and in all parts of the world. Numerous occupations offer us opportunities to fulfil our destiny. Consequently, there are many means available by which we can assist in increasing the prosperity of our Empire. It is obvious that we should encourage scientific research. But what shall we say to the problem of establishing the nation upon an agricultural basis, or a basis of commerce and industry, or yet on a basis which implies a parallel development of both? Upon what principles should we proceed to build up our trade? Is it necessary for us to establish colonies? How many important world-questions press for solution! What indeed are our true international obligations? What, again, are the occupations which we should adopt at home? We must be able to determine aright which among these various occupations that offer will be of true profit to society and to the nation. After all it is but natural that their number should increase with the development of the country. Finding ourselves in such a situation it is important that we should consider deeply, examine with care, and determine wisely as to those occupations which should be encouraged, those pursuits which are suitable to us as citizens of the Empire, and those activities which will result in the true prosperity of the Empire. Finally, is it not true that whole-hearted devotion to the occupation that we have chosen is the true and essential duty of every citizen of the Empire, and the fitting means of manifesting obedience to the Imperial Will?

CHAPTER XXV

National Institutions

SINCE the pillars of heaven were established and the strands of earth stretched firm the extent of heaven has been boundless and the greatness of earth past conception. Who can doubt the infinitude of the heavens or the limitless mass of the earth? In the midst of such phenomena our national institutions have been established and our laws promulgated. In such a setting the August Dignity of our Emperor shines in glorious effulgence upon earth as the sun and the moon adorn the heavens above with their beams. The people enjoy peace as the grasses and the trees enjoy tranquillity upon the surface of the land. Such phenomena are indeed a witness to the glory of our Empire. Who is there that would dare to question the august dignity of our Empire or the peaceful prosperity of our people?

The national institutions comprise the fundamental laws and regulations which should govern the country. In no instance does the national legal system extend beyond the limits set by these institutions. They provide the standards and the sanctions of the legal system. No contradiction can be permitted between them and this legal system. Is it not so clear as to be evident without proof in so many words, that all loyal subjects who recognise the necessity for the observance of the legal system, acknowledge and revere still more deeply those fundamental conceptions which are called the national institutions?

The Sacred Emperor above holds in his hand all the powers of government. Below him the whole nation of loyal subjects obeys his Imperial Will. The reason for the non-existence of the least dereliction in duties and obligations to the Sovereign on the part of the people is due to that mass of regulations which directs and regulates the deeds and the words of all. The national institutions indicate the lofty means by which the authoritative powers of the state may be set in motion. Even the ultimate authority of the Emperor is ordered by these national institutions.

The national institutions are the measure and the keystone of the national structure. The legal system is the ever-seeing eye of the state and the segments of its strength. Although national institutions and legal enactments take cognisance of different aspects of the national life their goal is one and the same. They are equally devised to secure the peace and prosperity of the nation. Therefore, the necessity for revering them is an essential which subjects can never afford to neglect, no matter what their circumstances. As national institutions comprise those fundamental conceptions which have reference to the authorities and powers of the state they are naturally to be found wherever a nation has been established. Irrespective of whether a nation happens to be an absolute monarchy or a republic, there always exists a set of national institutions which is in accord with the form of that state, forming the great basic law in every instance. It makes no difference whether the ultimate power resides in the one or the many, or in groups or parties. In all circumstances they are present. The existence of such institutions is a necessary phenomenon in every organised state. When we regard these institutions from a constitutional point of view it becomes evident at once that there is both a written and an unwritten law. Those institutions which are manifest in the written law are called the written constitution. The unwritten traditions we refer to as the unwritten constitution. Constitutions again are differentiated in the persons that grant them. Those granted by sovereigns are referred to as authorised constitutions. Those which are mutually arranged are known as federal constitutions. From this point of view our Constitution is a written and an authorised Constitution. In my view, however, it is not necessary to limit the national institutions to the national constitution. It is preferable indeed to assign a much wider significance to them. The authority of government which from ancient times has resided in the person of the Emperor can never be limited by any constitution. The powers defined in the Constitution are but one function of the authority of government. It can never be maintained that the Constitution

is the only function of the ultimate authority. When we recall
the fact that the authorities and powers of our Emperor are ever
unlimited and boundless there is no longer any room for confusion upon this point. Therefore, I have the temerity to regard
the significant word "kokken" which appears in the Imperial
Rescript on Education granted on the thirtieth day of the tenth
month of the twenty-third year of Meiji (1890) as having a much
wider significance than the term National Constitution in that
it relates to the whole mass of the fundamental institutions and
traditions of the nation.

From of old his subjects have ever revered the august
dignity and sublime virtues of our Emperor nor have they
lacked the abundant blessings of his radiant glory. In an ancient
book of poetry it is written,

On the occasion of the construction of the great palace, when the
plans under consideration were about to be carried into effect, the
people applied themselves so diligently to the work that it was com-
pleted in a short time. Although they were commanded not to be
in such haste they ran together all the more, as children gathering
about their father's knee.

In like manner do our people extol the lofty virtues of our
Emperor throughout their lives. Even the words of the poem
are inadequate to express that passionate devotion with which
they leap forward to obey his commands. Nowhere else upon
the earth is there anything that can compare with that complete
union of our four classes in devoted service to their Emperor.
The august benevolence of the Emperor extends to the four
quarters of the land. From the western shores to the uttermost
confines on the east there is no being that lacks refreshment from
the gentle dews of his benevolence. All are strengthened and
nourished by the winds of his grace. We must never forget that
it is due to the possession of such a peerless Emperor alone that
the three thousand years of our history have been as a flawless
golden vessel. It is for such a cause that it shall remain for ever
unalterable and immutable for a thousand and yet eight thousand

years. It is for such reasons that we stand alone in lofty isolation upon the eastern shores of the continent of Asia. It is for this cause that we have ever enjoyed great prosperity, constantly increasing our national prestige and displaying to all the world the peculiar and unique virtues of our national institutions. The source of this unparalleled renown which characterises our Empire is the firm establishment of our national institutions and the appropriate manifestation of the Imperial authority. There has never been any deviation in this regard from the correct path. It is due again to the fact that our subjects have ever known how to fulfil their duties and have constantly applied themselves with painstaking diligence to their occupations, without seeking to alter their proper destinies. It is due also to the careful maintenance of a proper distinction between high and low, and to the fact that the upper classes have never oppressed the lower, while they, on their part, have never envied their superiors. Our present renown among the peoples of the earth is, indeed, due to such facts as these. Who is there that loving his country does not at the same time revere the national institutions? We can never too greatly revere these fundamental national institutions whether we consider their content or their nature. Indeed the duty of rendering respect to the national institutions is so obvious that it requires no argument. Thus it goes without saying that every citizen applies himself both night and day to the realisation of these ideals and fears nothing so much as some dereliction in the fulfilment of his duties.

While mankind is prone to gather together into various groups the internal relations existing in those groups differentiate them and keep them separate. There are many varieties of groups, such, for example, as the family group, racial groups, social groups, and political groups. Each group seeks to maintain its independent existence. In order to secure this independence permanently they have on the one hand to fix the structure of the group and on the other to select certain written principles of organisation to which they will give allegiance. By means of such written articles the leader of the group is able to conceive the functioning of his authority and the members are enabled to fulfil their obligations. It is natural that each group should have its own articles of organisation which express its peculiar characteristics. Our national organisation consists of two groups, the higher and the lower. The first is the Ruler and all others are his vassals. Above there rules the Emperor who is possessed of all ultimate authority while below there exist his subjects who obey him. They fulfil his commands, they observe his wishes, and without neglecting anything apply themselves utterly to the accomplishment of his will. Since in our country all conceivable groups unite in and are derived from the lord and vassal relation it follows that the written articles of our institutions should on the one hand be related to the ultimate authorities existent in the Emperor and that they should on the other hand define the nature of the obligations of the subject. Should a subject, therefore, desire to fulfil acceptably the obligations imposed upon him, should he wish to follow the true Way of the subject without failure, he must be minutely acquainted with the true significance of the articles of our written institutions. It is only through a correct understanding of these institutions that we are enabled to fulfil the obligations of Shindo. Those who wish to fulfil the obligations of Shindo must first acquaint themselves adequately with the written institutions. They will then inevitably render true respect to the national institutions as a whole. Who is there among the subjects of our Emperor that fails to comprehend this truth?

The Emperor rules in august dignity above while at the same time the fundamental national institutions are manifest in glory. Below are the people firmly established in loyal service, observing their obligations as subjects, and endeavouring to fulfil the requirements of Shindo. We are blessed in such an Emperor, such fundamental written institutions, and such a people. Nothing is more firm than these pillars and foundations of our Empire. Nothing is more strong. Thus the pillars of heaven are set up and the sustaining ropes of earth are stretched.

Possessed of such elements as these the nation cannot help but rejoice in strength and vigour. It is but natural that our Empire should enjoy a glorious reputation, which resounds throughout the eastern heavens. How deeply should we who are subjects of the Empire revere these fundamental national institutions. Nor can we ever fail to laud the Imperial Destiny of our Empire, coeval with heaven and earth.

CHAPTER XXVI

The Laws of the Land

THE laws of physics are manifested in the workings of nature. The laws of the land depend upon the exercise of authority by the ultimate power. As all the phenomena of nature down to the smallest insect and the least particle of dust are without exception under the domain of law so too is every individual subject bound by the obligation to obey the legal regulations of his country. It is important to realise that in a nation, and by means of the proper functioning of natural laws on the one hand and human regulations on the other, all natural phenomena are well ordered, and the subjects of that nation are enabled to pursue their duties without confusion.

The legal regulations demand the absolute obedience of the subject and in their turn render him positive protection. By means of these legal enactments each subject's sphere of activity is fixed. By means of these regulations also the subject may learn the nature of his obligations. By means of these regulations he may avoid the errors of mutual injury. These benefits are all the result of the proper functioning of the legal system. If the subject observes the sanctions of this legal system he will be able to govern his daily life wisely and avoid all errors. The glory and virtue of our Emperor illuminates the whole earth, for the nation bows like the grasses of the field before the wind of his will as a consequence of the strict enforcement of the laws of the land on the one hand, and the painstaking efforts of all his subjects to render fullest obedience on the other.

The law of the land is omnipotent, whether expressed in the legal system or in all manner of regulations, decisions, and rules. Although the forms of its manifestation are not single its inner purpose is one, namely, the regulation of our lives. Our rights are fixed, our interests guarded, and our honour protected. Our whole lives should be determined in every particular through the functioning of these laws. Within the bounds set by them we are free to act and live and fulfil our destiny. Our property is safe and our rights are secured, our duties learned, our honour protected, and our interests guarded. If, on the contrary, the laws are not maintained, nor the regulations enforced, then, like a rotten pillar, the state will fail to sustain its honour, and the people will wander far from their obligations of service to the Throne. Recent alterations in social conditions within the Empire have led to the promulgation of a great variety of legal enactments. The words and acts of all loyal subjects should never exceed the boundaries set by these laws. They are the golden rules which must be obeyed and which we should carve deeply upon the tablets of our hearts. We should derive every detail of conduct from them even to the slightest lifting of the hand or the moving of the foot.

No human being regards his body as other than precious or his property as valueless. The respect rendered to honour and life is natural and the realisation of our peace and content is based upon these qualities. Should body or life suffer harm, should any one dare to injure these treasures, then the laws will punish the criminal. The victim is not required to secure the punishment of the wrongdoer directly nor to indulge in revenge.[1] Without the necessity of recourse to such individual action the laws will punish the criminal, judge him, and determine the degree of his guilt. It is the same with respect to injuries suffered in honour or property. The means of satisfaction are available. By these means property, honour, person, and life are protected. To go a step further the laws require positive action on our part in the form of military service and taxation. It is our duty to fulfil gladly all these obligations. These are indeed our duties as citizens of the Empire.

The law takes cognisance of our lives first of all in a negative manner when it sets up various prohibitions, and again in a positive manner when it requires various activities on our part. Sometimes it calls for a measure of voluntary action, again it demands unconditional obedience. Such, indeed, are the

---

[1] In 1873 the practice of katakiuchi or the vendetta was formally abolished.

functions of the national laws. The law is administered through a variety of departments. The law courts administer justice in cases of crime or in civil disputes. By such means the laws are effectively enforced and the innocent are not wrongfully condemned or thrown into prison. Thus the nation as a whole enjoys peace and safety and the blessing of the august grace of its Ruler.

The suppression and punishment of great and traitorous crimes is not the only purpose of the law. It is necessary to realise that the final object of the law is to secure the safety of the subject, to ensure the future prosperity of the nation, and to advance its wealth and power. If the will to obey is lacking in the subject disasters are sure to crowd upon each other in rapid succession, disputes will become endless, order in society will be destroyed, and a state of peace will become an impossibility. Let us take the case of the individual household. In a home where there is no fixed authority connubial bliss is impossible. No true fraternal spirit nor filial relation can exist there. If husband and wife fail to observe the proprieties the children will quarrel among themselves and it will be impossible to maintain the filial relation. These things are due to the fact that the domestic government which should unite the household and which should claim the obedience of all is defective. Thus the proposition that the peace of the household depends upon the firm establishment of domestic government is one that is easy to understand. Keeping this example in mind it is not difficult for us to realise that close relation which exists between the laws and the peace and safety of the nation.

For each and every one that has received the gift of life from this nation there is a natural duty, namely, to obey the laws of the country and to fear nothing so much as a possible dereliction in his obedience to these commands of the Emperor. As society becomes successively more complex so too the number of functions controlled by law increases. We must all carefully fulfil our obligations as citizens who exist under a constitutional government. To secure a parallel development with foreign countries and to avoid defeat in competition with them must indeed be our greatest endeavour. The laws govern all aspects of our conduct. Through them we avoid mutual injury and dishonour. Through a peaceful existence within the law we secure the future prosperity of the nation and serve our Lord acceptably. In this age when the number of legal enactments increases daily, when the activities controlled by law grow ever greater in number we should all realise that the cultivation of a knowledge of how to obey the laws and the training of our characters are essential duties incumbent upon all subjects of the Empire. To realise fully in practice such an obedience to the laws is truly our highest aspiration. I do not hesitate to declare that we have no other conception in this regard.

CHAPTER XXVII

Virtuous Courage

PRIMARILY, the impulse to regard property, honour, and life as precious, the desire to strengthen family ties and render parents a proper degree of respect, and the eagerness with which we seek to honour the Imperial commands, all arise from natural, innate tendencies implanted in our natures. They may also be said to arise from secondary social considerations such as the desire to secure greater prosperity for the individual, the fear of suffering dishonour, the wish to advance the true interests of the nation and to increase its prestige abroad. Phenomena of this nature are not merely confined to our past history, they live also in the present. In the moment of crisis our lives may seem of featherweight significance, and immense treasures as valueless as the dust. Confronted by a national emergency or summoned by the Imperial commands we forget all other considerations, even home and self. At such times we fear nothing save some imperfection or defect in our public service.[1] Such principles have ever been regarded as the sacred traditions of our people. Indeed, sentiments of this nature which would lead us to sacrifice the dearest honour and the most precious treasure, sentiments which impel us to leap to the defence of the country as water rushes to seek its own level, are the special pride of the people of Yamato and demand the most careful cultivation.

Courage in general may be divided into the greater and the lesser courage, into cultured courage and untutored courage. That courage is most highly praised which impels men to leap fearlessly upon the foe and which is, in the face of danger, invincible and unyielding. Such is the courage which in spite of great odds endures all hardship and advances with the irresistible momentum of the raging torrent. The courage which

---

[1] For General Nogi's marginal comments on this passage see Appendix, paragraph 22.

would fulfil its obligations in such wise as this is truly praiseworthy. The lesser courage, or what might be called the superficial or the mean courage, has ever been regarded with disdain.
Great men have scorned such courage. The spirit which would
throw itself with dauntless valour upon hardship has power to
move men and lead them on. Without such true courage mankind must wither and decay. Without such courage nations
become feeble and degenerate. In view of undoubted evidence
we are able to perceive that this spirit is truly the life-force of
humanity and the vital nerve of the national organisation. It
can never be too greatly stimulated. Such indeed is the greater
courage. Such is true courage. We should always bear in mind
that this is the type of courage possessed by all great men. How
truly is this greater courage to be revered! Since each subject
and each least handful of earth are the possession of our Emperor
no harm must ever be permitted to assail the one nor is any loss
to be endured with respect to the other. Loyal subjects of the
Emperor can never permit the injury of a single citizen nor the
loss of an inch of soil. From time immemorial our people have
never failed to observe the Imperial commands nor have they
neglected the protection of the national possessions. Subjects
of this Empire, which from its ancient foundation has never
witnessed the aggressions of foreign oppressors upon its shores,
scorn to display a mean or ignoble courage. Though possessed
of true courage they yet do not boast of it publicly. Nevertheless, when the august commands call forth their services they
spring valiantly forward to join combat with their enemies.
When the Imperial commands require their services they offer
themselves in invincible self-sacrifice regardless of life and
treasure, or of other things commonly held dear. They are ready
to devote the last ounce of their energy to the accomplishment
of their duties and to the fulfilment of their obligations, never
giving back a single pace but rather pressing forward with
resistless vigour.

Scorning all mean courage they seek to display only a truly
heroic valour. Avoiding untutored or savage courage they

devote themselves to the display of righteous courage on behalf of the public interest. This is not merely the duty of the faithful subject. It is an imperative obligation. The present world situation demands that these obligations be perfectly performed and their glory maintained in undiminished splendour. Unfaithful and unrighteous individuals who consider personal advantage and who seek to achieve selfish ambitions, without regard for nation or Throne, are utterly unworthy of our consideration. Those who understand the true significance of virtue and who comprehend the meaning of honour must fling aside spade and hoe, and grasping their weapons firmly, forsake private aims and devote themselves to the public service. They must neglect private wrongs and consider only the cause of the nation. Such persons will avoid error and will acceptably fulfil the obligations of righteous courage. They will thus consistently display those precious virtues which have never been lacking among the loyal subjects of this Empire. To devote one's self unreservedly to the public good, to serve the Imperial will without thought of person or family, of wife or child, or yet of old friends; and when questions of public service arise to put forth the last ounce of energy, mutually contending in self-sacrificing service while fearing nothing so much as some dereliction in that service, are not these indeed the true heart impulses of the loyal subject? From of old the subjects of our Emperor have served the interests of the state with righteous valour, never bringing dishonour upon Lord or nation. Those who have a true understanding of our history can be in no doubt as to these statements. It is the dearest wish of fifty million hearts to be worthy of the honour of perpetuating such virtues for ever.

In this age when education has become so vital and culture advances with each succeeding day, when in the mechanical world, and in the spheres of science and theoretical learning, new inventions and refinements are by no means scarce; in this age when the means of communication are so highly perfected that the whole world seems united in a single unit of co-opera-

tion, we cannot afford to neglect the most strenuous pursuit of
self-cultivation for a single day. Should we take a false step,
should we fall behind the rest of the world in culture, then no
matter how beautiful our spirit, no matter how courageous our
valour, displayed in the service of the state and burning ardently
within our bosoms, no matter to what degree we may strive to
realise the true and full value of our courage, no matter with
what devotion we may apply ourselves to the great tasks of
public service, we must inevitably display some palpable inferiority. One manifestation of courageous valour offered
acceptably to the public service is that it shall parallel in the
nation the daily progress of the world's cultural advance. To
realise the best results we must develop the necessary moral
ideals and at the same time encourage the study of all essential
subjects. We should clearly grasp the importance of gaining a
mastery of the more important subjects. While clearly perceiving that virtuous valour displayed in the public interest is
not limited to the passing day we must at the same time ensure
that a high degree of such service shall always accompany and
parallel our present progress in culture. The virtuous valour
which our citizens aspire to display is this type of courage and
no other.

CHAPTER XXVIII

The Imperial Destiny

WE cannot afford to neglect or despise the merest handful of earth or the least cupful of water. Ravening wolves with insatiable appetites are ever ready to pounce upon anything which chances to be unguarded. As hungry tigers that contend over their prey the nations of the earth glare angrily at one another. This is the situation in which we find ourselves to-day. There is no unoccupied region left where men may break new ground with plough or hoe, nor are there new seas for the fisherman.

Although from one point of view the sphere of international relations has suddenly become greatly extended it has also, through the development of mechanical devices, become greatly contracted. This contraction has brought to the fore certain unfortunate aspects of the wretched drama of human misery. The evil of hypersensitiveness seems to increase continually among the nations. When the storm clouds gather in eastern Europe the alarm bells begin to ring in eastern Asia. A threatening situation in North America disturbs the peace of northern Europe. A discarded scrap of flesh upon the Asiatic continent has power to assemble the hungry vultures from the whole earth. If a piece of bread is thrown out in southern Europe it has power to assemble the ravening lions from every region. The veriest scrap of flesh or portion of bread exposed, even in the most distant corners of the earth, has power to throw the whole world of men into wildest confusion. Why is it that the degeneration of humanity proceeds apace? Certainly justice is dispensed, morality urged, and benevolent teachings of all kinds recommended. Unfortunately, however, such things are only effective in a limited sphere and to a strictly limited extent. Truly, the countries of the world cannot rest in safety behind their boundaries. Human kind cannot afford to put its trust in the mere enforcement of moral precepts. It is only when we have the strength to repulse our strongest enemies that we can in tranquillity sing the praises of peace. Is this not a true description of the present situation? How unfortunate is this state of affairs!

From the southern littoral to the confines of the north communication by shipping of all types is abundantly available. With the increased facilities of transportation no place remains inaccessible to the human foot. The smoke of human habitation ascends in every corner of the earth. Who would dispute this marvellous expansion of humanity in modern times. Equally extensive and universal, however, is the fact of human strife. If those who are neighbours engage in mutual assault and strive to prey upon each other's domains, occupying themselves continually with quarrels as inconsequential as the combats which snails wage with their horns, they are liable to be oblivious of more serious perils. They are in danger of neglecting the enemy who hides in the darkness behind and the ambushed foe who stands black-masked with ready sword. If we should be fortunate in defeating the first foe we may nevertheless fall a victim to the second who lurks hidden behind. Human history abounds in examples of this kind. We must always consider well the causes which have on the one hand led to the success and prosperity of nations and on the other brought about their downfall and destruction. It almost seems from the many examples that are available that heaven has decreed that no nation or society shall escape the fate of periods of greatness and prosperity followed by downfall and decay. How striking indeed are these extreme vicissitudes of human history! Eventually, even the prosperous mulberry grove may give place to the conquering ocean. On the other hand yesterday's deeps may become the shallows of to-day. We should never neglect considerations of this kind. Such phenomena are familiar to all who review with care the history of Europe, nor is there any doubt that Asia presents a parallel case. What a sad and wretched fate! Among all these nations of the earth what people is there that is possessed of a uniquely different history? What nation stands aloft and superior to all the rest of the world fulfilling its destiny with calm dignity upon the shores of the Pacific? How proudly we reply, the Empire of Japan! Has it not ever been a deeply rooted aspiration among the people of Yamato, an ideal handed down by the ancestors through successive generations, to consider nought but the service of the Empire and the maintenance in perpetual prosperity of the Imperial Throne? I rejoice in the glorious and assured future of our Emperor and of his people.

The inviolate perpetuation of the Imperial Shrines, the advancement of the public interest, and the constant increment of the wealth of the whole people are without doubt the fixed objectives of the statesman and the fervent desire of every citizen. Nevertheless, I am filled with wonder when I consider how rare is the actual realisation of such objectives in the unbroken fulfilment of a myriad successive epochs. Though the world is wide indeed and nations many in number none is truly worthy of our unqualified praise. Though there are peoples in great variety none is worthy to be our model. Alone among these teeming multitudes of the earth our Empire exhibits its peculiar pre-eminence. None but this Empire of ours can boast of three thousand years of history wherein the maintenance of the Imperial Shrines has been uninterrupted, wherein the prosperity and power of the nation have been steadily increased, whose course has never deviated from a steady approach to the distant goal of all her progress. In the remotest antiquity our Toyo-Ashi-Hara Land was united and the ever unalterable Imperial Destiny was set forth and firmly established, at the very foundation of the state. From the eastern provinces to the confines of the west all his subjects are for ever refreshed and sustained in the sea of the Emperor's authority, and never withhold their praises of his benevolent government. The spirit of Yamato has shone undimmed from the earliest age and the constant beauty of that virtue of service to the Emperor, which all observe and in which all hearts unite, has continued to shine like a lovely gift granted by heaven above. Thus we have escaped all dishonour abroad, while at home each and every one has devoted himself with diligence to his peculiar task. Thus from the dawn of history to the present day we have never suffered foreign aggression nor yielded an inch or a foot of territory. Are we not justified in our self-confidence in view of these facts? Truly here the heavens are content, earth rests in peace, and the Ruler governs a happy people. Do not these words well describe the ideal and peaceful reign? In very truth these have been the elements composing the living history of our Empire. How fortunate are we who possess such a history?

As of old so to-day, it is true that the nation guards its possessions with jealous care. Nevertheless, should the least opening be afforded, our enemies will struggle to the death, utterly regardless of the sentiments of others, in order that they may satisfy their insatiable hunger by pouncing upon a small area of water or morsel of territory. The nostrils of those who review human history are assailed by the polluted winds which sweep from piled-up corpses. They are forced to hold their noses in the presence of the awful stench of human deeds. This is the common experience of those who review the history of human affairs. In the midst of this abominable desolation the Imperial dignity shines in brilliant and unalterable effulgence. The unbroken succession of our Dynasty has ever shone with the unchanging radiance of the sun and moon. The Imperial Destiny fills and refreshes all the land. The people enjoy due prosperity and serve their Imperial Family. Is there in the whole earth a nation comparable to ours?

An examination of the precepts of Tokugawa Ieyasu[1] rewards us with these sayings,

The life of man resembles the undertaking of a distant journey while engaged in carrying a heavy burden. Haste is to be condemned. When we consider that insufficiency is the lot of man we are not dismayed by misfortunes. When we desire some luxury we should

---

[1] Although it is generally held that the Legacy of Ieyasu with its hundred chapters of precepts and practical policies was written by an eminent scholar long after the death of the great founder of the Tokugawa Shogunate, it may be taken that it "substantially reproduces the spirit of his policy" (Murdoch). Great emphasis is placed upon loyalty throughout and the "way" of the samurai clearly indicated in a host of pungent aphorisms.

recall the days of our indigence. Patience is the basis of a tranquil and happy life while anger is an enemy. If we know only how to win and not how to lose we shall not escape disaster. Judge yourself rather than others. It is always better to underdo a thing than to overdo it.

Truly these words make clear his conception of life. In this age, however, I believe that we cannot rest satisfied with such a view. In this day when we are obliged to cross fiery mountains and tread upon mines of high explosives we cannot help concluding that conditions are different. We tremble when we pass in review the formidable history of mankind. Nevertheless we alone are able to stand in the midst of this stage of humanity, filled as it is with unutterable suffering and woe, and calmly cultivate the beautiful realisation of our virtues while fortifying our courage. In a land utterly his to the utmost lonely beach, where in the most secluded spot none but his retainers dwell, in a land where Biwa's pellucid waters reflect beauty to the skies unaltered by the succession of a thousand autumns, in a land where sacred Fuji ever exhibits in lofty and superior grandeur its peculiar virtues, from generation to generation all things unite to manifest the everlasting glory of the Imperial Destiny. We should realise that it is our glorious destiny to serve our Emperor as long as sun and moon endure and heaven and earth persist. There can be no higher honour or happiness for us than such service as this. There is, indeed, no end or limitation to the Imperial Destiny which is coeval with heaven and earth.

CHAPTER XXIX

Patriotism

ACCORDING to a certain venerable classic

The ancient rulers who desired to exhibit superior qualities in the conduct of national affairs governed their countries with extreme care. Such as desired to succeed in government first gave attention to the ordering of the household. Those who wished to procure well-ordered households first gave the most careful attention to self-cultivation. Those who wished to attain the ideals of self-cultivation endeavoured to attain uprightness of heart. Those who desired an upright heart cultivated a true will. Indeed from Emperor to common man it was acknowledged that all worthy achievements centred in such self-culture.

Since self-culture gave rise to an epoch of peaceful prosperity and good government it is obvious that nothing is more important in heaven and earth.

By the grouping of individual units families are established. By the grouping of families the nation is formed. As the nation resembles the family group so do all the people unite in the sentiment of love of country, in the same manner as the individual loves his home. Since to love one's self is an innate and natural impulse even the uncultured and the uneducated respond to it. Self-love is an innate tendency which enables men to achieve position in the world. Developed and enlarged this self-love becomes love of family and love of home. In its fuller manifestation it becomes love of country or true patriotism. Such is, indeed, the logical consequence and the natural development of the human impulse of self-love. Men who are moved by self-love and who desire to enjoy a long and prosperous life do not limit the impulse to themselves as individuals but extend this love to family and home. Again, there is considered to be no safer way of securing a complete realisation of self-love than within the national organisation.

Thus the contentions that true self-culture in the individual will result in peaceful prosperity and good government in the nation and that the impulse of self-love is the ultimate basis of that patriotism which ensures the greatness of the nation, are generally held to be true. Although true self-culture and true self-love are undoubtedly desirable things yet I cannot admit the theory that peaceful prosperity and good government must of necessity arise from the display of a superior self-love on the one hand or the achievement of an exalted self-culture on the other. I believe that there is no strictly logical connection between this exalted self-culture and self-love on the one hand and peaceful prosperity and good government on the other. On the contrary I believe that there is a palpable hiatus here. If we carefully consider the past history of our nation, if we review our characteristics and achievements with care I am sure we shall find that our ideals have always differed radically from those of other nations.[1]

On the fourth day of the first month of the fifteenth year of Meiji (1882) the Emperor himself graciously instructed the Army and the Navy in the ideals of the warrior in the five word motto which he bestowed upon them, namely, "Loyalty, discipline, valour, probity, and frugality". He decreed that they should endeavour to realise these ideals in a spirit of sincerity. That warriors should endeavour to obey the Imperial command goes without saying. Such endeavour, however, is not limited to our warriors. Every Japanese subject to the inhabitant of the humblest hovel must inscribe these words deeply upon the tablets of his heart and obey the Imperial command in fear and trembling. What a true ideal is this! How lofty an ideal is this that we should all unite in mutual emulation and in the equal display of true loyalty to the Emperor and true service to the Imperial House!

Patriotism is described in a word when we say that it devotes its whole strength gladly and without reserve to further the

[1] For General Nogi's marginal comments on this passage see Appendix, paragraph 23.

interests of the country and when we say that it is instant readiness to sacrifice life and fortune in the service of that country, without one backward glance or least regret. The heart which is filled with patriotic sentiments ever perpetuates the observance of the national ceremonies and guards the Imperial Shrines, while devoting itself to the realisation of the eternal destiny of our country. A careful examination will show that the nature of this concept of patriotism is not necessarily always the same. Although the history of every nation abounds in accounts of valorous deeds and patriotic self-sacrifice a slight analysis will serve to show that for the most part these deeds were conceived for selfish ends or for the aggrandisement of some particular clan. Or else we find that the ideal of nationality or national unity was invoked to satisfy personal ambition. Patriotism even though displayed in a mere mechanical service or out of deference to custom is always worthy of praise. The patriotism of the citizens of this Empire, however, differs in quality from that found in all other countries. The patriotism of our Imperial people is manifest in that keen endeavour to obey and respect the commands of the Emperor to the last and most minute detail. In very truth from the humble peasant to the last city dweller every citizen is born to serve and if need be to die for our Emperor. This ideal of service to the Throne is a special characteristic of our nation which exists nowhere else in the world. This ideal, which from the foundation of the nation has ever pervaded the land, is truly one of the most beautiful of our characteristic and innate possessions.

In our Empire the Emperor is the state. The Emperor is one substance with the state and shares its destiny. All service on behalf of the nation is service to the Emperor himself. Without the Emperor there could be no state. Reverence toward the Throne and patriotism in respect to the state have the same object and goal. Reverence to the Throne and patriotism must have the same significance. From the foundation of the Empire our people have served the Emperor obediently and rejoiced in his paternal care. They have never turned aside from the true

Japanese Way of loyal service to country and Emperor. An ardent patriotism and a devotion to the Throne, wherein the Emperors of the unbroken and inviolate Dynasty constitute the central object, are the innate and peculiar possessions of every citizen. There is, therefore, nothing astonishing in the fact that the Japanese ideal should be superior to that of other nations.

Patriotism is a Japanese ideal and is manifest in reverence to the Throne and love of country. This spirit is ever present in the daily unfolding and the progressive realisation of our auspicious destiny. The impulse is expressed through the medium of loyalty, filial piety, connubial accord, friendship, faith, correct conduct and a myriad other virtues. Although it is not to be limited yet if we would express it in a word we may call it Nippon Shindo, and say that it signifies two things, reverence to the Throne and loyalty to the Emperor. Hence the whole duty of the subject is to observe and obey the commands of the Emperor. With the Restoration our country took its place among the group of the great powers. At home we applied ourselves to a more intensive development of agriculture, commerce, and industry, while abroad we made it our object to build up trade. At home we perfected the elements of civilisation while abroad we applied ourselves with care to the establishment of diplomatic relations. In all our activities we desired to be well-pleasing in the sight of our Emperor. We must never forget that we have a great future before us and that we must apply ourselves earnestly and put forth every effort in order to realise our destiny and fulfil the obligations of loyalty.

To fulfil our obligations to the Emperor and to devote ourselves to loyal service, these are the beautiful ideals of our people. We call this Yamato-damashii.[1] Yamato-damashii means loyal service to Emperor and Throne. It is a spirit which refuses to yield under severest trials or even to death itself. Indeed Yamato-damashii is that thing which, moving along the way of Nippon

---

[1] "The Spirit of Yamato", a highly symbolic term which embraces a wide range of qualities and traditions held to be peculiarly Japanese. See also note on page 23.

Shindo, produces the effect called true loyalty. This spirit of loyalty and service to the Throne is the innate possession of every Japanese citizen without distinction of rank or station. It is equally the possession of samurai, farmer, artisan, and merchant. Possessed of this Yamato-damashii they all serve the Empire to the limit of their treasure and their strength, without one self-ward thought.

Loyal service and self-sacrifice for a great cause are not the unique possession of our people. Such qualities characterise all men. In the days of Sparta's greatness, or when the renown of Alexander the Great resounded through Europe and Asia, or again when the might of the Emperor Napoleon shook Europe to its foundations the profession of arms enjoyed great prestige. In our country also men like Dōkyō, Masakado, and Takauji flourished exceedingly for a brief period. Although many were loyal to them such loyalty differs radically from that inculcated in the way of Nippon Shindo. Yamato-damashii follows the way of Nippon Shindo and seeks to fulfil our immutable destiny. That loyalty was merely temporary but this is eternal. That loyalty was evanescent but this is enduring. Yamato-damashii makes loyalty to the Emperor central. Patriotism of this nature is its central principle and is implicit in its advance along the way of Nippon Shindo. Citizens of Japan, full of the spirit of Yamato-damashii, have ceaselessly kept the true path of Nippon Shindo from the very foundation of the Empire. Hence there can be no least doubt that the Imperial Throne of our Emperor coeval with heaven and earth shall enjoy an ever-increasing prosperity and that the nation, following the true path of loyalty and patriotism, shall continue to shine with ever-increasing glory.

CHAPTER XXX

The Way

AFTER three months of vernal spring wherein the blossoms of peach and plum are rivals in beauty and the cherry blooms in pride a flaming radiance bursts suddenly upon us so glowing and ardent that it seems to melt the very metals, and men find themselves in the midst of that season whose heat is not to be borne. When the leaves of the paulownia fall to the earth, when the zenith recedes to immeasurable distance, and the well-fed horse browses in the fields our spirits grow tranquil and our minds are refreshed. Again the aspect of nature alters and six-petalled snowflakes dance in the sky while storm winds vaunt their power abroad. That season is at hand when the pine displays his peculiar virtues in the wintry landscape. Thus have the four seasons alternated for a myriad epochs unchanged. Thus in the wide and boundless universe cold comes and heat. Thus harvests are gathered in autumn and stored in winter. This is in truth the way of nature and of man. How shall we who are citizens of the Empire live successfully in the midst of these changing phenomena without a true Way to guide us and a safe resort?

Opportunities for the development of industry and the increase of national wealth throng upon us. Methods of agriculture are improved and the five grains are produced in rich abundance. With each passing day the amenities of life are more perfectly realised. Herein is the vital development of mankind manifest and the auspicious destiny of society fulfilled. Nevertheless, if men in the enjoyment of warm clothing and a sufficiency of food content themselves with a state of idle luxury and neglect the teachings of morals they will become but little better than wild beasts, they will be ignorant of correct manners and without understanding of the respect due to elders. Such men will be unworthy of the name, and such a nation will exhibit few characteristics of true manhood. Given conditions such as these society can hardly escape destruction. It is for this very reason that the Way must be taught. In teaching the Way questions of morality are of the utmost importance. By their aid correct relations are established between parent and child. By this means the maintenance of the correct relation between Emperor and subject is assured. By such teachings the separate functions of husband and wife are determined. By means of the elder and younger brother relation correct manners are maintained. By such precepts is mutual trust between friends encouraged. Through moral teachings primitive man was fashioned and led upward and forward. The Way is, indeed, the final essence of the teachings of sages and philosophers. All citizens of the Empire endeavour by day and by night to offer the fruits of filial piety to their parents, to sustain the relations of true fraternal life between brothers, to achieve that connubial ideal wherein the husband proposes and the wife acquiesces, and to realise the lofty ideal of good manners in mutual trust between friends. Are not these the very qualities which establish our Empire as a model for the whole world?

The man who wears coarse clothing and adopts a frugal style of life is easily misunderstood. He is often despised and regarded as a barbarian or an unprogressive person. The man with a robust spirit who concentrates on the realisation of a single ambition is regarded as proud and reactionary and may even be ostracised by society. The man who observes the proprieties and cultivates virtue is blamed for his bigotry. The economical man who applies himself closely to his affairs is often regarded as a miser. The man who loves wide human contacts and who seeks the praise rendered to benevolence[1] is frequently called a hypocrite and a flatterer. The man who applies himself to the pursuit of learning, to the mastery of a profession, to the cultivation of his intellect and to the perfection of his character is often discriminated against as an ignoble creature and a hypocritical opportunist who is merely seeking means to increase his own

---

[1] For General Nogi's marginal comments on this passage see Appendix, paragraph 24.

popularity. Men who devote themselves to the public good or spend their whole lives in the service of the state are often attacked on the ground that they are sacrificing the nation to personal interests. Can we not all recognise these tendencies as the common defects of the world in which we live? The fact that the citizens of this Empire are unique among the peoples of the earth in freedom from such tendencies, the fact that they alone among all nations are able to display such lofty and superior qualities is due entirely and in every instance to the teachings and the grace of our Emperor.

Questions of liberty, natural rights and other similar theories continually exercise the minds of men. As a result there may even appear those who would rise in armed revolt against their rulers. There may appear men who hold the laws in disdain and who indulge in rioting. Examples are not wanting in the records of foreign nations. Indeed they exist in a state of constant turmoil occasioned by chaotic subversions of government. Our Empire stands aloft and superior to all such tendencies, follows no false bypaths, and advances steadily towards the further shore of its destiny. This is possible because our citizens constantly honour the Imperial edicts, revere the fundamental principles upon which the state is founded, and obey the laws.

When the true flag is unfurled and the loyal troops advance what soldier is there that lacks in gallantry or in courage? Careless of the corpses of the fallen piled in heaps, heedless of rivers of blood flowing on every hand we concentrate only upon the fulfilment of the Emperor's commands and the duty of sacrificing ourselves in the realisation of his designs. Is this not the reason why our soldiers are superior to all others upon the Asiatic continent? Is this not the reason why they are held in high regard by all the peoples of the earth? While our past history, from the most ancient times, has been rich in these qualities, the recent events of the Sino-Japanese War of Meiji twenty-seven and twenty-eight (1894–1895) also carry on the tradition with honour. Who was it that severely chastised that great and excessively proud Empire of China, and caused its countenance to blench, when, proudly conceiving that it was the central flower of civilisation, it displayed its arrogance in the possession of mighty dominions and cruelly oppressed the eight provinces of Korea? From what country were those soldiers who came to the aid of the hardpressed representatives of foreign powers upon the outbreak of the Boxer Rebellion? To what country did those soldiers belong who aroused their wondering admiration? These great deeds were, indeed, due to the sacred virtues of our Emperor and the loyalty of his subjects. The renown we acquired was the natural consequence of that loyal spirit which is the special characteristic of the people of Yamato. The impulse to fulfil their duties and to realise the eternal Imperial Destiny is due to this quality and none other.

How marvellously the glory of this Way radiates to the eight regions of the earth, filling the four seas! From of old the citizens of our Empire have ceaselessly followed it, nor will they ever forsake or neglect its sanctions. Neither at home nor yet abroad has its glorious renown ever suffered impairment. This fact indeed justifies our pride. It goes without saying that future generations of subjects will cherish such ambitions and so conduct themselves that they may never bring disgrace upon their ancestors.

How glorious is the destiny of our Emperor which shall for a thousand epochs maintain its lofty pre-eminence and still remain the object of human veneration! It is due to qualities of this nature that our Empire is able to maintain a unique and superior position among the nations of the earth. There is no subject of the Empire but longs to observe the commands of the Emperor with the utmost devotion and loyalty, willingly rendering life itself should the occasion demand. Let us recall the fact that our Empire has marvellously displayed its pre-eminence in eastern Asia, that it has demonstrated its valour before all the world, and that it has secured the respect of all nations by its deeds. By means of such ideals we the subjects of that Empire have ever served the mighty design. I have therefore no hesitation in declaring that while sun and moon stand in the heavens and earth continues to revolve beneath the foot of man it will ever be our highest happiness to offer our all in the service of the Emperor. What boundless happiness we should feel in the possession of such a Way and in the constant effort to realise it! Whether in the distant past or in the future the subjects of the Empire have but one ambition. They aspire to follow the Way in sleeping or in waking and in every possible circumstance.

By reason of these ideals we advance over mountains and cross rivers fearless of dangers or of the thorns of the thicket. Through obedience to the Emperor we are able to enjoy the manifold privileges of this Empire in safety and to pursue our occupations in the midst of an earthly paradise. Not only are we permitted to dig our wells and to drink their waters in safety. Not only can we till our fields in peace. The very heavens are filled with clouds of blessing while on earth human proprieties are carefully observed. The glory of the sun and the moon is constantly renewed and we rejoice to sing the praises of this happy age. In the midst of such blessed and harmonious surroundings we live in unconscious accord with the will of our Emperor. Such is a true description of the conditions which govern our lives. Above there rules a sacred Emperor, while beneath there exists a people from of old rich in the virtue of loyalty. Such being the case it is but natural that great deeds should characterise our past, while in the present age, following the Way without deviation, loyal subjects of our Emperor are able to fulfil their obligations and to ensure the prosperous destiny of all elements in our national life. Furthermore, there can be nothing surprising in the fact that we have been able to unfurl the banner of success upon that mighty field of competition, the sad world in which we live. How glorious is the future of all who follow this Way! We must ever acknowledge with all reverence that our good fortune is due to the august grace of our Emperor.

POSTSCRIPT

I SHOULD like to indulge in a few reminiscences as I conclude the task of correcting the proofs of the "Nippon Shindo Ron". As I lay aside my brush I cannot help recalling some of the circumstances of the past fifty years of my life. Stimulated by the kindness of General Nogi, as expressed in his words of advice, I am encouraged to devote still greater energy to the propagation of this Way. Although conscious of my own insufficiency I have nevertheless devoted half of my life to the education of the young of this country. It has been my life-work to secure a sound mind and a healthy body in the young by devotion to the inculcation of Nippon Shindo and the encouragement of athletics. That I have been able to do a little good in these two directions causes me endless satisfaction. The pleasure I have in this accomplishment calls to mind memories of my former teachers, my parents, and my elders. Moved by such considerations I have placed their photographs at the beginning of this volume.[1]

My late elder brother Oda Hajime while seeking to realise still loftier ideals of service passed away at the age of fifty-one, on the twenty-first day of the ninth month of the third year of Taishō (1914). When I reflect on the half of my life which is passed and look into the future, when I recall memories of my late brother and consider the years to come in which I shall be deprived of his companionship I am overwhelmed with sadness. I have chosen to write a memorial of my brother because of this sorrow which oppresses me and because it will furnish an opportunity of recalling once more memories of my former teachers, my parents, and my elders.

Viscount Kaneko who was closely connected with my late brother in public affairs and an intimate friend in private life said of him:

He had an extremely penetrating mind and was a man of great and decisive determination of character. He was also an administrator of

---

[1] Omitted in the English edition.

rare ability. Though his will was exceedingly strong his sympathies were broad. He practically forgot himself in his efforts to serve the interests of his friends and his official inferiors. I had privately made up my mind to leave my affairs in his hands when I passed away. How sad that the opposite has turned out to be the case! To him alone could I have entrusted the care of my growing family.

My brother must be comforted where he lies beneath the sod by these sincere words of his friend. Truly he was the leader among the men of learning in the Oda family. My eldest brother Ryō, a former representative to the Diet from the Prefecture of Aichi, my younger brother Keishu who is now head priest of the old temple of Chōbo, and my other younger brother Yasunaga, now known as Doctor Suzuki, all have sought to emulate him. (In the family I was second to my late elder brother. There was another younger son called Sukenobu who died at an early age. I have also an elder sister Hatsuno who is living at the present time.) Through his influence and aid we each received our education. My elder brother derived his characteristics of industry and determination from his father. He was very like his father in character, and his father favoured him most among the brothers. Although he was by no means prone to attend to the wishes of his children he was nearly always ready to listen to my late elder brother. I have often heard from my own former teacher Mr Tatematsu of the great diligence of my elder brother when he was a pupil in the primary school. Through his great application to his studies he often had occasion to receive special favours at the hands of his teacher. The example of uprightness set by his aged father Fuginobu and the affectionate care of his mother Koharu were much out of the ordinary. I remember to this day the familiar appearance of my brother after he began to attend the middle school. He used to make the round trip of six ri (c. fourteen and a half miles) from his home at Kusakabe trudging in indigo-coloured shorts and straw sandals through the rice fields, in order that he might return home every day. Simplicity was the keynote of his whole life. When he later came to enter the University he was the first from Nakashima County to do so.

After graduating from the Law College and while taking a postgraduate course he lectured in the Higher School and at the Special Law School. He became an official of the Department of Home Affairs in the twenty-fourth year of Meiji (1891). Later, at the recommendation of Viscount Kaneko he became a secretary of the House of Peers. In the twenty-seventh year of Meiji (1894) he was sent to Germany where he studied first at the University of Berlin and later at Heidelberg. Whatever time he was able to spare from his courses he devoted to a study of the organisation of a house of representatives, in accordance with the wishes of Viscount Kaneko, and diligently forwarded the results of his research to the Viscount. When, at the conclusion of the War of twenty-seven and twenty-eight, the Viscount became Vice-Minister of Agriculture and Commerce he requested my brother to prepare a survey of the post-war administration and financial policy adopted at the conclusion of the Franco-Prussian War. The results of this research were published in the form of a book which was issued by the Department of Agriculture and Commerce and presented to Prefectural Offices, Chambers of Commerce, and leading business organisations. In the year twenty-nine my brother became an official of the Department of Agriculture and Commerce, and in thirty-one he was appointed Private Secretary to the Minister. At the same time he was also appointed Councillor of the Department and Councillor of the Court of Administrative Litigation. Later he was sent to China on an official mission. In June of the thirty-third year he was appointed a Commissioner of the Fifth National Industrial Exposition which was held at Ōsaka. His appointment as Special Commissioner in the year thirty when our country took part in the Paris Exposition was the beginning of these activities. After the Ōsaka Exposition he was, in thirty-six, appointed Chief Commissioner of the Japanese Section at St Louis, and in thirty-eight he became Chief of the Bureau of Patents. In forty-one he went

to Seattle again as Chief Commissioner. Thereafter he was
appointed Chief of the Bureau of Agriculture and became a
Councillor of "chokunin" (Imperial appointee) rank. Until he
fell as the result of excessive labour he devoted the greatest
energy to the organisation of expositions and to the supervision
of patents. To such an extent was this the case that the idea of
expositions became inseparably connected with the name of Oda.
He devoted all his energies to enhancing the prestige of Japan
and to the introduction of her culture into foreign countries.
It was due to him and a group of his friends that "The Collection
of Japanese Arts and Crafts" was published with a view to
recording the finest achievements of Japanese art and making
them accessible to the world at large. Finally, with Viscount
Kioura he organised the Society of Inventors and devoted much
energy to this new department. Mr Shimura, President of the
Industrial Bank, a former classmate of my brother and lifelong
friend has said,

He was a democratic man, and as an official even carried to excess his
fondness for intimate relations with ordinary people. This was one
of his strong points. His outstanding success in the missions to the
foreign expositions, his marvellous gifts as an authority on expositions
in Japan, his excellent service as head of the patent office, and the
great encouragement and stimulation which he was able to render
to the Society of Inventors were due to this outstanding characteristic.

We must thankfully acknowledge the high praise of his
intimate friends. Viscount Katō, his elder in the home community, who arranged my brother's marriage, said of him, "He
is a man with a great future". Although the work which he
accomplished can fortunately never be lost, it is nevertheless a
great pity that this "man with a great future" could not have
served his country for a longer period. As one of his brothers
I am overwhelmed with sorrow at this thought.

I have chosen to employ the opportunity of the republication
of this book, "Nippon Shindo Ron", to add these thoughts
regarding my late brother. Fortunately, all his brothers are

living still and are in the enjoyment of good health, and it is our hope that we may be able to render effective service for many years to come. The insignificant but honest impulse of my heart thus revealed in "Nippon Shindo Ron" has received great encouragement from that god-like man General Nogi. I shall never cease to devote all my feeble energies to the perfection of the ideals of my fellow-countrymen. In publishing this book it gives me great pleasure to acknowledge with thanks the assistance of those eminent educators Mr Tomisaburo Hattori and Mr Motosue Ishida.

The twelfth month of the ninth year of Taishō.

Signed by the Author.

The Marginal Comments of
General Maresuke Nogi

A FTER careful consideration it has been decided to place the marginal comments of General Nogi in an appendix rather than to attempt to print them on the margin of the appropriate pages as in the Japanese edition. The different arrangement of the English printed page has rendered this change imperative. In the Japanese edition the General's comments were reproduced exactly as he had written them with the brush at the margins of the printed matter.

A word of caution is perhaps not out of place to the occidental reader who may not be familiar with the more intimate aspects of Japanese life. In referring to General Nogi's comments it should be borne in mind that he jotted them down in the margin while reading the book for the first time. They are not in any sense carefully considered judgements or criticisms of the contents prepared with a view to publication. A reference to the correspondence included in the introductory matter will serve to show that this was the General's own estimate of them. There is, however, an undoubted value in spontaneity. General Nogi by reason of his qualities and his commanding position has become the foremost representative in the new Japan of those characteristics which were until recently the chief prerogatives of a dominant and exclusive group. In an important sense he is the symbolic mediator of these characteristics in the radical rearrangement of groups which has not yet reached a point of stability. The attitude of General Nogi to the main thesis of this work is, therefore, of very great interest. The belief that the comments, brief though they are, will be of real service to the occidental student has led to their inclusion in this form.

No attempt has been made to reproduce facsimiles of the General's notes, as the arrangement of the original material does not lend itself to effective reproduction on the English printed page. For facsimiles of the General's handwriting the reader is referred to the two letters included in the introductory matter. The General's script has been reproduced in the Appendix in the form of the usual printed symbols and arranged in a manner suitable for easy reference.

(Tr.)

Comment No. 1, page 12.

傍 ト ハ 何 ソ ヤ 痛 戒 ヲ 要 ス

"What is meant by 'in addition to' (katawara)? This usage deserves criticism."

General Nogi evidently objected to the use of the word "katawara" in the original which might imply that the military arts were of secondary importance. (Tr.)

Comment No. 2, page 12.

現 時 ヲ 云 フ カ 將 タ 明 治 以 前 ヲ 云 フ カ

"Is this a reference to the present or to a period prior to Meiji?"

Comment No. 3, page 36.

忠 哉 忠 哉 日 本 臣 民 ノ 道 義 ハ 皆 之 ヨ リ 出 テ 之 ニ 歸 セ サ ル 可 ラ ス

"Ah, loyalty, loyalty! How true it is that all the virtues of the Japanese subject arise from this source!"

Comment No. 4, page 40.

亞 洲 ト 云 フ ヘ キ カ 寧 ロ 地 球 ト 云 ハ ン ノ ミ

"Should we speak of Asia alone here? We should rather refer to the world as a whole."

General Nogi evidently objected to the description of Japan as a mere part of the Asiatic continent. (Tr.)

Comment No. 5, page 43.

文字屢杜撰多キヲ惜ム

"The frequent employment of unnecessary verbiage is regrettable."

Comment No. 6, page 48.

至言々々

"How true!"

Comment No. 7, page 49.

日本臣民タル孝ノ本義實ニ此ニアリ
テ存ス

"This is indeed the true conception of filial piety held by the Japanese people."

Comment No. 8, page 49.

然リ

"True!"

Comment No. 9, page 49.

敬服々々

"Admirable, admirable!"

Comment No. 10, page 58.

見識雄大

"What a noble conception!"

Comment No. 11, page 58.

一ナラサレハ德ニ非ルナリ

"Unless it is single it is not virtue."

Comment No. 12, page 64.

如何

"Question?"

Comment No. 13, page 66.

福音ハ我未タ識ラサルナリ

"The use of this word 'fukuin' (good news or glad tidings) is unfamiliar to me."

Comment No. 14, page 76.

超絶的ト應急的ノ教育我レ初メテ之ヲ聞ク夫何ソ奇ナル

"This is the first time I have ever heard of super-education and education which adapts men to the requirements of the age. It strikes me as peculiar."

Comment No. 15, page 78.

教育家抱負應ニ此如クナルヲ要ス

"Educators should cherish this ambition."

Comment No. 16, page 79.

同感

"I concur."

Comment No. 17, page 97.

交游ヲ愼ム

"The selection of friends requires the most painstaking care."

Comment No. 18, page 99.

友愛

"This indeed is true friendship."

Comment No. 19, page 122.

Although General Nogi did not write out a comment against this paragraph he drew in the margin the Japanese brush mark for emphasis. As this is reproduced in the Japanese edition mention is made of it here. (Tr.)

Comment No. 20, page 125.

智德別途ノ説服スル能ハス俗ニ云正直ノミヲ以テ德ト云ヘケンヤ智仁勇ヲ兼備シテ德初テ顯ハル

"I cannot consent to the separation of wisdom and virtue. Honesty is popularly conceived to comprise virtue. Nevertheless true virtue is only apparent where knowledge, benevolence, and courage are united."

Comment No. 21, page 127.

公德私德ヲ云フノ人ハ德ノ何タル知ラサル卑人ノミ

"People who talk about public and private virtue are fools. They are ignorant of the true meaning of the word."

Comment No. 22, page 147.

日本臣道ノ定義ナリ

"This is a true definition of Nippon Shindo."

Comment No. 23, page 157.

然リ唯忠アルノミ

"True, there is nothing beside loyalty."

Comment No. 24, page 162.

是卽チ僞ナリ奸ナリ

"This is wicked hypocrisy."

It is evident that General Nogi objected to the words "homare wo uken to su", which might be rendered "one who *seeks* to gain a reputation" for superior benevolence, etc. (Tr.)

For EU product safety concerns, contact us at Calle de José Abascal, 56–1°, 28003 Madrid, Spain or eugpsr@cambridge.org.

www.ingramcontent.com/pod-product-compliance
Ingram Content Group UK Ltd.
Pitfield, Milton Keynes, MK11 3LW, UK
UKHW012347130625
459647UK00009B/596